MW01482102

Messiah

The Story of Jesus According to Matthew

**A STUDENT HANDBOOK
INCLUDING A NEW PARAPHRASE
OF THE GOSPEL OF MATTHEW
WITH ATTENTION TO THE ORIGINAL LANGUAGES,
ALONG WITH ILLUSTRATIONS, MAPS,
AND NOTES**

Don R. Camp, M. Div.

© 2015 Don R. Camp

All rights reserved. This book or any portion thereof
may not be reproduced or used in any manner whatsoever
without the express written permission of the author
except for brief quotations in a book review.

**Contact the author at
drcamp06@gmail.com
drcPublishing
Tacoma, Washington**

Printed by CreateSpace in the United States of America
North Charleston, South Carolina, USA

First Printing 2016

ISBN-13: 978-1523669592
ISBN-10: 1523669594

Cover illustration is a painting by Antonio Ciseri titled *Ecce Homo.*

Table of Contents

Author's Foreword

Messiah: The Story of Jesus According to Matthew is a handbook to the Gospel of Matthew. It includes a paraphrase of the Gospel, illustrations and maps that make the land of Jesus understandable to the reader, and footnotes that aid the reader in understanding Jewish customs and the background of these in the Hebrew Scriptures.

The author's comments in each chapter are intended to help the reader understand the message of the Gospel of Matthew and the intent of Matthew as he presented the words and life of Jesus the Messiah to his Jewish readers - and to us.

Each chapter is enriched by a master artist's interpretation of one event included in the chapter.

The paraphrase of the Gospel of Matthew is in boldface type to set it off from the author's comments. The purpose of the paraphrase is to make the story of Jesus accessible in the same way the J.B. Phillips *New Testament in Modern English* made the Bible accessible to the author as a teenager. The paraphrase attempts to make Matthew's story of Jesus flow like a modern narrative with events connected, where it seemed appropriate, with transitional words or sentences. Many of these transitions are not in the Greek text but are added for readability.

The Greek text of Matthew and the Hebrew text for many of the quotations from the Hebrew Scriptures were consulted in the preparation of the paraphrase. But every paraphrase is an interpretation. For that reason the author approached the task of paraphrasing Matthew with seriousness and prayer, not wanting to misrepresent the inspired words of Matthew.

Additional background to the book of Matthew and to the author Matthew follows in Background to Matthew.

Chapter 1
Family History

Joseph's Dream by Gaetano Gandolfi, 1790.

Every man in the land of Judea knew who he was. If asked, he could answer: I am a son of Jacob (or Matthiah, or Zacharias). I am from the tribe of Benjamin (or of the tribe of Levi, or the tribe of Judah). And I can trace my family back through the list of the heroes of Israel to our father Abraham. Every man knew who he was.

Jesus was the same. He had a family. And the heroes in his family were many. They included all the kings of Israel clear back to David, the greatest king. The heroes included Judah and Jacob and, of course, Abraham.

paraphrase

1-6. We begin the story of the Messiah Jesus with his family. He was a descendent of King David, and both he and David were descendants of Abraham. This is the line of descent: From Abraham to David there were Isaac and Jacob and Judah (and his brothers) and Perez and Zerah (their mother was Tamar). Then there were Hezron and Aram and Amminadab and Nahshon and Salmon and Boaz, whose mother was Rahab. Boaz's son was Obed, whose mother was Ruth. Then there was Jesse, who was the father of David the king.

7-11. After David there was Solomon. He was David's son. His mother was Bathsheba, who had been Uriah's wife. [These two men were the kings of the united kingdom of Israel.] Solomon's son was Rehoboam. Then, continuing the family line, there were Abijah and Asa and Jehoshaphat and Joram and Uzziah and Jotham and Ahaz and Hezekiah and Manasseh and Amon and Josiah and Jechoniah and his brothers. [All these were kings of the southern kingdom of Judah.] At the time of Jechoniah the people of Judah were taken away as captives from the land of Judah to Babylon.

12-17. After the Jews returned to Israel following the captivity in Babylon, Jechoniah had a son named Shealtiel. His family continued through his grandson Zerubbabel and then through Abiud and Eliakim and Azor. Then there were Zadoc and Achim and Eliud and Eleazar and Matthan down to Jacob, who was the father of Joseph the husband of Mary who was the mother of Jesus, the one who is called Messiah (Christ). There were fourteen generations from Abraham to David and fourteen more from David to the time when the nation was taken in captivity to Babylon. And there were a

final fourteen generations from that point to the birth of Jesus the Messiah.

Matthew's purpose was to show that Jesus is the Messiah. (The word *Messiah* is translated into the Greek language by the word *Christ*.) Matthew began by connecting Jesus to the prophecies of the Messiah found in the Hebrew Scriptures (our Old Testament). Here in this list of names Matthew connected Jesus to Abraham and by implication to the promise made to Abraham in Genesis.

"I will make you into a great nation,
and I will bless you;
I will make your name great,
and you will be a blessing.
I will bless those who bless you,
and whoever curses you I will curse;
and all peoples on earth
will be blessed through you."
Genesis 12:2, 3 (NIV)

The connection to Abraham would grab the attention of every Jew. The Jews were fiercely proud of their heritage as children of Abraham and heirs of the promise.

Paul the Apostle, for instance, who was himself a Jew from the family of Benjamin, referred to this pride of ancestry as something he once cherished.

"I myself have reasons for such confidence. If someone else thinks they have reasons to put confidence in the flesh, I have more: circumcised on the eighth day, of the people of Israel, of the tribe of Benjamin, a Hebrew of Hebrews..." Philippians 3:4-7

However, Matthew was not simply trying to impress his readers with the fact that Jesus was a son of Abraham; every Jew was a son of Abraham. He wanted to show that Jesus was a son of David, for that was an essential qualification for Messiah. By his relationship to David, Jesus would have an ironclad claim to the title of King.

18-21. Now, this is how the birth of Jesus happened: While Mary was engaged to Joseph, before they were married, Mary became pregnant with a child. It was a miracle of the Holy Spirit. Joseph, Mary's fiancé, was a man who had always done right.[1] He did not want to endanger or

embarrass Mary, so he planned to end their engagement by divorcing her privately.

Even Joseph - maybe especially Joseph - was sure that Mary had done something very wrong. Whoever heard of a girl becoming pregnant without sleeping with a man? It could not happen! No, this was a disgrace. But Joseph was a good man. He didn't want to harm Mary. So he decided to end their engagement quietly and not make this a messy, public exposure that would endanger Mary. Since engagement was very much like marriage, divorce was the option that allowed Joseph to do what was right and still protect Mary. He would not have to explain why he was divorcing her.

But while he was thinking about this, an angel appeared to him in a dream. The angel said, "Joseph, you who are a son of David, don't be afraid to take Mary as your wife. Her child is from the Holy Spirit. She will have a son. Name him Jesus because he will save his people from their sins."

The name Jesus was a common name. In the Hebrew language it is Yeshua, or in English Joshua. Joshua was the name of one of the Jews' greatest heroes. Joshua was the man who led the Israelites to conquer Jericho and to possess the Promised Land. Boys in Jesus' time were named Joshua with the hope that they might grow up to be famous like the first Joshua. Maybe they too would save their people like that first Joshua. And everybody knew that the people needed saving. All they had to do was look around. Roman soldiers were everywhere. Herod, their so called king, was a man placed in that office by Rome. And he was an evil man. Yes, they needed saving. They needed a new hero. But to save them from their sins? That was a new idea.

Or was it? Prophets in the distant past had told of the coming of a special man. These prophecies can be found in the Hebrew Scriptures (the Old Testament), and they date back thousands of years. In all, there are over 300 of these prophecies. Some like Isaiah 53:5,6 speak of this man to come as taking their sins upon himself. So people were not taken totally by surprise. But it is true they didn't have a really good picture of what this Messiah would be like. Some thought he might be a military leader. Some thought he would be a new king. Some even had the idea that he would lead the people back to God.

22-23. All this happened to fulfill the words written by the prophet Isaiah: *"Look, now a virgin will be pregnant."*

Why is it important that Mary be a virgin? In addition to allowing that Jesus be both divine and human, there is another reason. Paul explains in Romans 5:12 . A member of a family shares the benefits and obligations of the family. If the head of the family owed a debt, everyone in the family shared the obligation of that debt. Paul's point is that all people are children of Adam, the first man and the head of the human family.

It follows then that because Adam sinned, the debt of guilt for sin passed to all his children; they are all sinners. That includes all of us because we all are related to Adam. If Jesus had been born into Adam's family line by having a human father, he would have inherited Adam's debt of guilt for sin, just like a debt is inherited by a son if his father dies without paying the debt.

If Jesus had been born of a human father, he could not have been the father of a new family line, a family line that did not bear the debt of guilt for Adam's sin.

But Jesus had no human father, and thus had no guilt. He could be the father of a new family, a family of people who are adopted into Jesus' family. These people owe no debt; they no longer carry the guilt of Adam's sin because they are members of a new family.

"She will give birth to a son who will be called Immanuel." (That means God with us.) [2]

Matthew then wrote that this Messiah would be "*God with us.*" That's what one of the prophets in years past had said: "*His name will be Immanuel.*" And that is what Immanuel means: God with us. So, as *God with us*, saving from sins is not out of the question; God can do what we cannot.

24-25. After the angel had spoken, Joseph got up from his bed and did what the angel told him to do; he took Mary as his wife, but he did not have sexual relations with her until she gave birth to her son. And Joseph named him Jesus.

God among us. So, what will this man who is God among us be like? What will he do? What about this saving from sin? How? That is what Matthew will tell us in this book, The Gospel of Matthew.

FOOTNOTES

1. The unfaithfulness of an engaged woman was legal cause for punishment. That punishment could have included death. But Joseph decided to divorce Mary. Divorce saved her from punishment and was also legal.

2. Isaiah 7:14. Some have suggested that using Isaiah's prophecy to prove that Mary was a virgin fails because the word in Isaiah can just as well mean a young woman. But the word can also mean a young virgin. Yes, the prophecy was, first of all, about Isaiah's wife, who was a young woman but not a virgin. However, the prophecy had an additional fulfillment. That fulfillment had to do with Mary, who was both a young woman and a virgin. In any event, Matthew put it plainly that Mary had never slept with a man.

Chapter 2
A Tumultuous Beginning

The Magi Journeying (Les rois mages en voyage), James Tissot,
late 19th century. Brooklyn Museum

How could a baby be a threat to a king? It is true King Herod had murdered enemies and potential enemies and even his own sons to make sure no one could take his power and place as king. But a baby? A baby didn't pose any threat.

Of course, Herod was crazy. Literally.

1-2. Jesus was born in Bethlehem in Judea, the Jewish region of Palestine, while Herod the Great was king. After his birth, astrologers, who are called Magi,[1] came from the east to Jerusalem. They asked, "Where is the one who has been born king of the Jews? We saw his star and have come to worship him."

Had a new king been born? Was it true? If it was, that was a threat to Herod. But he knew what to do. No one could stop him. It is not surprising that the people of the Jew's capital Jerusalem were troubled. What evil could this king do? Indeed, what evil would he do? He would certainly end this threat as he had ended every threat, even if this baby was the rumored Messiah the Jews were always talking about. He would kill him.

But why would Matthew include this story in his Gospel? Because, the fact is, the Messiah King does challenge the political and social establishment. Every follower of Jesus has a higher allegiance than to his nation or king or president. He owes allegiance first of all to Jesus.

It also reminded Matthew's readers that such hatred toward the Messiah should be expected. Psalm 2 predicted it:

"Why do the nations conspire,
and why do the people plot in vain?
The kings of the earth rise up
and the rulers band together
against the LORD and his anointed, saying,
'Let us break their chains
and throw off their shackles.'"

3-4. Herod was disturbed when he heard this and all the people of Jerusalem with him. When he had gathered all the chief priests and Jewish Bible scholars, he asked them where this "Messiah" was supposed to be born.

4-6. They told him that he would be born in Bethlehem of Judea because that is what the prophet wrote: *"Bethlehem*

in the land of Judah, you are in no way the least important among the cities of Judah. From you will come a ruler who will shepherd my people Israel." [2]

Matthew is the only one of the four Gospel writers to include this story of Herod and the Magi. He did so in order to show how the birth of Jesus fit the Hebrew Scriptures' prophecies of the Messiah.

7-8. Herod called the Magi to meet with him, but he did this secretly without the knowledge of the priests or scholars. Herod wanted to find out when the Magi had first seen the star. Then he sent them to Bethlehem. He commanded, "Go and find the child, and then come back and tell me so I too can go and worship him."

So the Magi continued on their journey. The Jewish teachers said that Bethlehem was the place where the Messiah would be born. Bethlehem was only six more miles.

9-12. The Magi listened to Herod and went to Bethlehem. The star they had seen while they had been in the East showed them the way and finally came to rest above the place where the child was. When they saw the star, they were filled with joy. When they entered the house and saw the child with his mother Mary, they knelt down and worshiped him. They then opened the gifts they had brought – gold and frankincense and myrrh.

The star led them to a house in Bethlehem. When they entered the house, they found a mother with a young child. And they knew they had found the one they had been seeking.

Matthew's account of the infant Jesus did not include his birth in a stable as did Luke's. That suggests that the Magi arrived sometime after the birth of Jesus and after Joseph and Mary had found a house in Bethlehem.

The Magi gave him the gifts they carried with them. The gifts were appropriate: gold for a king, incense as a symbol of divinity, and myrrh as a reminder of mortality. Though the gifts might well have been usual for any king born during this time, they proved to be particularly appropriate for this child king: He was indeed a king, the King of kings. He was truly divine. And He would die on a Roman cross for the sins of the world.

What about the star? It has been the subject of debate and speculation ever since the science of astronomy has been able to rewind the movements of the stars and planets and determine what the skies might have looked like at any particular date in history. Though there have been those who have speculated the star was a super nova or an alignment of the planets, there has been no answer that is absolutely confirmed by science. It is probably best to accept that the star was a miracle.

The star, however, was more than a miracle. It was a fulfillment of prophecy, as was the visit of the Magi. In Numbers 24:17 there is a cryptic and ominous prophecy spoken by Balaam fourteen hundred years earlier regarding the people of Israel and the people of Moab. The people of Israel were on their forty-year journey from Egypt to the land God had promised to them. Nearing the end of that journey, they crossed the land of Moab where Balak the king of Moab hired the prophet Balaam to curse Israel. Balaam, however, did not curse Israel. He could not, for God would not allow it. Rather he blessed them and predicted that it would be Moab that would be destroyed at some time in the future.

In that prophecy Balaam says, *"I see him, but not now; I behold him, but not near. A star will come out of Jacob; a scepter will rise out of Israel."*

The prophecy predicted a future king from Israel who will crush Moab (perhaps a symbol for all who oppose God). This future king, Matthew declared, is the one who was born in Bethlehem and whose birth was announced by a star.

The Magi who followed the star were probably from Persia. They were not Jews. They represent the nations. In Genesis 49:10 Jacob predicted that a king would come from the descendants of his son Judah and that the nations would obey him. This baby king was that one, and the bowing of the Magi before him pictured the ultimate obedience of the nations to the Messiah.

The inclusion of the Magi also introduced to Matthew's Jewish readers an idea that will become more and more significant through the book. That idea is that the Messiah is a Messiah for all people. That is clearly revealed in the Hebrew Scriptures, especially in the book of Isaiah. But it was not an idea that would have been comfortable for the Jews of Jesus' day. They had become convinced that they alone were God's chosen people and that people of other nations were not.

That resulted in a deep division between the Jews and people of every other race. But in Jesus the division is ended. Matthew's Jewish readers needed to realize that.

But having been warned in a dream not to go back to Herod, they returned to their own country, avoiding Jerusalem.

Of course, Herod caught on when the Magi did not return. But he knew enough. It did not matter if he did not know exactly which baby in Bethlehem to kill; he would kill them all. He sent his soldiers with orders.

13-15. After the Magi left Mary and the child, an angel appeared to Joseph in a dream and told him, "Get up. Take the child and Mary and leave right away for Egypt. Stay there until I tell you, for Herod is going to search for the child to kill him." Joseph immediately got up and took the child and Mary that night and left for Egypt. He stayed there until Herod died. This fulfilled the prophet's words: *"Out of Egypt I have called my son."* [3]

Joseph and Mary and the child Jesus were gone by the time the soldiers arrived at Bethlehem. And Herod didn't get another chance. He himself died shortly after.

The death of Herod in 4 B.C. helps establish the date of Jesus' birth. The birth had to be earlier than the death of Herod. It might have been as much as two years earlier, but it is more likely that it was a year or less. That would give us an approximate date of 5 B.C. for the birth of Jesus.

16. When Herod realized he had been tricked by the Magi, he was very angry. He ordered that all the boys who were two years old and younger in Bethlehem and in the whole region around Bethlehem be killed. He decided on that age because of what the Magi had told him about the first appearance of the star.

It was awful. But it was nothing Herod had not done before.

17-18. That fulfilled the words of the prophet Jeremiah: *"A voice could be heard in Ramah, crying with loud wails of grief, Rachel crying for her children; and she would not be comforted because her children were dead."*[4]

The prophecy about Rachel crying for her children is not an example of quote mining. (Quote mining is the practice of finding a quote somewhere that can prove the author's point, even if taken out of context.) No, Matthew knew the context of the quote and what it would mean to his Jewish readers. [5]

The quote comes from the book of Jeremiah. The verse refers to the return of the Jews from captivity in Babylon. Matthew understood that the renewal of the nation at the return from Babylon was a type or a foreshadowing of the ultimate return of the nation to the Lord that will happen at the end of this present age. But it began with the coming of the Messiah described by Matthew. His readers would know the context and understand the larger meaning of the quote: the murder of the babies of Bethlehem was an example of the oppression God's people would suffer as they waited for Messiah and for the spiritual and national renewal of God's people.

19-23. After several years, however, Herod died, and an angel came again to Joseph in a dream. The angel told Joseph, "Take the child and Mary and return to the land of Israel. Those who tried to kill the child are dead." So Joseph did what the angel said, returning with the child and Mary to Israel. But when they arrived, he heard that Archelaus, Herod's son, was king in Judea, and Joseph was afraid. However, he was directed in a dream to find a home in the region of Galilee, and he took the child and Mary there to a small village called Nazareth. This fulfilled what had been spoken by the prophets that the Messiah would be a Nazarene. [6]

Joseph and Mary returned to their own land. They had been told by an angel in a dream that it was safe. But to be really safe they did not return to Bethlehem, rather they went back to Nazareth where they had lived before. It was a nothing kind of town. No one would expect to find a king in Nazareth, even if they were interested enough to look. And no one was.

FOOTNOTES

1. Magi were professional astrologers or astronomers who were part of a priestly class in Persia. The wise men who advised Nebuchadnezzar in the book of Daniel were probably of this class. Daniel may have been considered among the Magi, and it may have been through Daniel that these Magi in Matthew came to know of the star that was to come out of Judah. See Numbers 24:17

.

2. Micah 5:2-4. The quote in Matthew combines parts of Micah 5:2 and 4, but the quote is not a literal translation of the Micah verses.

3. Jeremiah 31:15

4. Hosea 11:1

5. There is actually a word to describe a short quote that is intended to remind the reader or hearer of the larger context. It is *remez*.

6. There is no direct quote in the Old Testament for this reference. Some think that Matthew was making a play on words, something like what we would call a pun, since Nazarene is close to the word Nazirite. A Nazirite would be a person dedicated to God. Samson, for example, was a Nazirite, a man dedicated from birth to God. See Judges 13:7

Chapter 3
The Testimony of God

Jesus (left) is being identified by John the Baptist in John 1:29.
by Ottavio Vannini, 17th century.

Everyone called by God for a work, whether king or priest or prophet, needed the anointing of the Holy Spirit. David, for example, was first anointed with oil by Samuel in 1 Samuel 16:13, and then he was anointed with the Holy Spirit: *"the Spirit of the Lord came upon David from that day forward."*

Would the Messiah need the anointing of the Holy Spirit? Yes, even though he was the Son of God, he had not come to act independently, and the anointing of the Spirit and the affirmation of God from heaven indicated that he would not be acting independently. His works and his words as the Son would be the works and the words of the Spirit under the direction of the Father.

This is how it happened.

1-3. While Jesus was yet in Nazareth, John the Baptist began to preach in the wilderness east of Jerusalem and along the Jordan River. His message was this: "Change your ways. The time of the kingdom of heaven is near." John was the man Isaiah the prophet spoke about when he said, *"A voice! It is crying out in the wilderness: 'Prepare a path for the Lord; make his pathway straight.'"*[1]

4-6. John's clothing was made of camel's hair with a leather belt around his waist. His food was locusts and wild honey. And many people came out from Jerusalem and, in fact, from the whole region of Judea to hear him, and he baptized many in the Jordan River as they confessed[2] their sins.

John's clothing, life and message would have set him apart from almost everyone else and would have indicated to the Jews, who knew the manner of such men from the past, that he was a prophet. He would have been a magnet who would have drawn crowds of the curious as well as the serious.

His dress and life said something about his character and spiritual life. He was definitely not part of the religious establishment. The Pharisees, priests and the Sadducees, who were the religious establishment, dressed in fine clothing that advertised that they were the elite. John's clothing said that he was a man who was not interested in playing that game. He was interested in only one thing, and that was not popularity or the easy life. It was to speak God's message to the people of Israel.

7-10. However, when John saw that many of the Pharisees and Sadducees[3] were coming to be baptized, he warned

them sharply, "You snakes! Who told you to escape the anger that is coming? If you are serious, show by your lives it is real repentance. And don't fall back on the old, empty claim that 'We have Abraham as our father.' I tell you, God is fully able to turn these rocks into children of Abraham. Look! The axe is ready to chop down the tree, starting with the roots. Every tree that does not produce good fruit will be cut down and thrown into the fire."

There is sometimes a debate about whether faith in God's grace - that is, God's pure undeserved forgiveness based only on God's goodness - or the works of faith is the key to salvation. Those who emphasize grace often quote Paul in Galatians 2:8 where he says *"You are saved by grace through your faith."* Those who emphasize works will quote James 2:17 where James writes *"faith if it is not accompanied by works is dead."*

It is best to understand that faith and works, such as those John the Baptist demanded of the Pharisees, work together; one is not complete without the other. So it was appropriate for John to tell these men to get their act together and live as God desired them to live. That would show that they really did believe.

11-12. To the crowds, John cried out, "I baptize you with water because you've said we are changing our ways and turning to God. But the one who is coming is far greater than I. His shoes I am not even worthy to carry. He will baptize with the Holy Spirit and fire. So beware. His hayfork is in his hand, and he will thresh the wheat, gathering the grain into the barn; but the straw and chaff he will burn in the fire that will never be put out."

John was a fiery preacher. He was not afraid to call out people who were hypocrites and fakes and to tell them of God's coming judgement on their sin. No one would contest that. In the end that fearlessness in speaking the truth is what got him killed. But here John was speaking of the Messiah.

John was saying that there was coming a judgment, which in a metaphor he calls fire. The Jews would all agree with John to that point; they could read that in the Hebrew Scriptures which spoke in many places of God's judgment. The prophets of the past - Isaiah, Joel, Malachi and many others - had all spoken God's words of warning. But John's point was that it is the Messiah, the one whose coming John was announcing, who would gather the wheat, the righteous ones, and burn the straw and chaff in the fire. That implied that the Messiah would be the final word and the final judge. That equated the Messiah with God. That was a new idea.

Matthew's readers knew about John. He had been a prophet with a reputation for speaking God's message fearlessly and with clarity and power. Even Flavius Josephus, a Jewish historian who wrote seventy years later about the history of this time, wrote about John's reputation. And Matthew's Jewish readers, more so than even Josephus, still respected John. So if John declared that the Messiah was the ultimate prophet and judge, that carried some weight.

But what about this Messiah? Matthew was clearly identifying him as Jesus. But is he going to judge? (John metaphorically called judgment "thresh the wheat.") Is he going to burn the worthless chaff in the fire?

Many today prefer to see Jesus as "meek and mild." The picture we have here pictured in John's words doesn't seem to fit that image.

What is the truth?

The fact is, Jesus was meek and mild. He did not come blowing a trumpet and drawing attention to himself. He did not come to condemn. The Apostle John wrote in his Gospel in chapter 3:18 that "*God did not send his Son into the world to condemn the world but that the world might be saved.*"

That work of saving, however, required that people face their sin. And that required that harsh truths be spoken. In this sense, no prophet spoke the truth more clearly than Jesus, and no prophet spoke of the consequences of sin more soberly. He spoke not merely of the destruction or the judgement of the nation; other prophets had warned of that. Jesus spoke of eternal judgment. That is sobering to anyone who takes his words seriously. But his purpose was not to pass judgment; it was to save. So it was in hope of the repentance of the sinner and his salvation that Jesus spoke.

But the Bible is also clear that when Jesus returns at the end of this age, he will come as the judge of evil men and evil institutions, and his judgment will be severe on those who have hardened their hearts toward him and to the truth he spoke. John's warning was not prophetic hyperbole: "*The axe is ready to chop down the tree.*" We should not hope in Jesus' kindness if we are unwilling to turn away from sin and place our trust in him.

13-17. Now while John was preaching on the banks of the Jordan River, Jesus came from Galilee to be baptized. But

John objected saying, "I need to be baptized by you rather than you to be baptized by me." But Jesus replied, "Let it be done, for it is good for us to do what is right." To that John agreed, and he baptized Jesus. As Jesus came up from the water, the heavens opened, and he saw the Spirit of God coming down to rest on him as a dove, and a voice spoke from heaven and said, "This is my Son whom I love and with whom I am pleased."

Why was it "right" for Jesus to be baptized? Because it was an act identifying himself with men. He had no sin to repent of, it is true, but to be our Savior he had to "empty himself." He had to set aside for this time his glory and his rights as God the Son. He would now be wholly dependent upon the Father and upon the Spirit's anointing. (Phil. 2:6-8)

The Son of God's self-renunciation meant that he would live as fully human. He would thirst. He would hunger. He would hurt. He would die. It was not an act. It was real. And that allowed him to give his life in exchange for us. It allowed him to be our Savior.

Jesus identified himself wholly with men by his baptism, but at the same time there could be no more certain evidence that Jesus was the Son of God and Messiah than this word from God that followed his baptism. It was God the Father's endorsement. The anointing of the Holy Spirit would now enable him to fulfill his ministry as Messiah Prophet. And those who were there saw and heard it all.

FOOTNOTES

1. Isaiah 40:3. The quote from Isaiah, as with almost every quote Matthew included in the book, needs to be seen in its larger context. In Isaiah 40 the short verse Matthew quoted is part of a wonderful promise of comfort and hope. Every Jew hearing these words would know the passage in Isaiah and would understand that John's message promised the forgiveness of sins and their restoration to God as his well-loved people.

2. "Confession" meant that they deeply realized and admitted that they were sinners and that God's judgment of sin was right and just. It was also an appeal to God's mercy, for that was their only hope.

3. The Sadducees were men of the wealthy elite and priestly class. The High Priest was typically a Sadducee. But they also were the political leaders of the Jews. Many on the Sanhedrin, the Jewish court, were Sadducees. Of course, the Romans had installed kings over the Jews, and there was a Roman governor, but the Sadducees were the political leaders within the nation. The Pharisees were the theologians and religious teachers.

Chapter 4

Tempted and Affirmed

Christ in the Wilderness by Ivan Nikolaevich Kramskoi, 1872

Jesus fit the prophecies of the Messiah King in the Hebrew Scriptures. He was affirmed by God at his baptism to be the Son. He was qualified by the anointing of the Spirit to be the Messiah Prophet. There remained only that he be tested. How firm was his commitment to submit to his Father and to his Father's will?

This chapter will show that he was single minded in that commitment.

1-3. After this, the Spirit led Jesus up into the wilderness and he was tempted by the devil. When Jesus had fasted forty days and nights, he was extremely hungry. That is when the tempter came and said, "If you are really the Son of God, make these stones into loaves of bread."

The writer of Hebrews 4:15 tells us that Jesus the Messiah was tempted in every way we are tempted. That seems incredible to us. How could Jesus have been tempted in every way we are tempted? And why? He was the Son of God. How could God be tempted?

That's a good point, of course. God can't be tempted. James tells us that in James 1:13. But Jesus the man could be tempted. He could be hungry and desire food. And in this first test, Jesus faced this very temptation. Would he choose to use his power to satisfy his appetite? More pointedly, would he use his power to satisfy his appetite rather than rely upon God the Father to provide for his needs.

This temptation is ours too. Will we choose the easy road when God's will is the hard road, the road where God's power can be seen in our lives? Will we be ruled by our appetites, whether those are for normal and otherwise acceptable things, such as food, or whether they are forbidden and harmful, such as sexual sin or greed? Or will we choose to be ruled by God?

4. But Jesus replied, "Life does not depend on bread alone, but on what God provides in his plan for us."[1]

Jesus chose to rely on his Father's provision and plan for his life. It was the choice to trust God, even when things are not comfortable. His choice was not super human. We can make that choice as well.

The second temptation tested Jesus' humility.

5-6. Then the devil took Jesus to Jerusalem, the holy city, and to the topmost part of the Temple. He said to Jesus, "If you are truly the Son of God, jump off; for it is written in the scriptures 'God will command his angels to carry you,

so that you will not so much as stub your foot against a stone."[2]

7. Jesus again replied, "It is also written, '*Do not test the Lord your God.*"[3]

Jesus again chose the Father's way. But Jesus' reply, a quote from the Hebrew Scriptures, prompts us to ask what *test the Lord* means. In the context of Deuteronomy 6, the passage Jesus quoted, it meant don't complain about what God has provided for you. That may have application to this temptation since it was again a choice to submit to God's way of humble submission to God's provision of protection when it was truly needed.

But there is something else going on as well. The devil introduced this challenge with the word *if*. It was like saying: "So you are the Son of God are you? If you think so, let's see. Throw yourself off this high place and see if God rescues you."

Jesus, of course, knew who he was. The devil knew as well. Jesus was also sure of God's promise of protection. This was not about finding out who he was. So, this suggestion by the devil was a taunt. It was an appeal to egotism and pride. It was an appeal to show off. But there was no egotism. There was no need to show off. There was simply peace. Who he was would be proven legitimately often enough in the days ahead.

We too are faced with appeals to our ego. We forget that we are loved by God. We want the love and attention of others. So we show off. We brag about ourselves. We one-up others when they get the attention we crave. We want life to be all about us, and we forget that God's love is all we need.

The third temptation appeals to Jesus' holy desire that the kingdoms of the world be his to rule.

This was, of course, the destiny to which he was born. It was the will of the Father from eternity that the Son of God would rule. But it was also the Father's will that his rule be characterized by laying down his life for the sake of those he ruled. So the question in the test was whether Jesus the man wanted the place of power and authority so much that he would turn from the Father and the Father's way and worship the devil to gain it - and thereby avoid the cross.

8-9. Finally, the devil took Jesus to the top of a high mountain from which he could see all the kingdoms of the world and their magnificence and said to him, "I will give

you all of these if you will bow down and worship me."

10-11. Jesus replied, "Get out of here, Satan! It is written in the scriptures, *'Worship the Lord your God and serve him and him alone.'"*[4] At that the devil left him, and angels came and helped him.

Satan's offer, though rejected by Jesus, will be offered again and again through history. It is offered to us. Will we sell our souls to the devil to realize our dreams? Is there something, anything, we want so much that we will have it in disobedience to God's will in my life? There was nothing Jesus wanted so much that he would reject the Father's will and plan.

In First John 2:16, John summarized the inner sources of temptation as *"the lust of the flesh, the lust of the eyes, and the pride of life."* Jesus was tempted at each of these points, just as we are tempted. (The lust of the flesh was his first test. The lust of the eye was his third. And the pride of life was the second.) The temptation Jesus underwent probed every moral nerve. And he chose the will of the Father in each one.

But why the temptations at all? Was it not certain that Jesus would triumph over temptation? He was God after all. Yes, but he was also a man, and the temptations, which were very real to the man, connected him to our experience of temptation.

A priest's ministry is to represent men before God. The writer of Hebrews tells us that in order to minister with compassion a priest must relate to the weaknesses of men; he must know what it is to be tempted. Jesus' temptation qualified him for the office of Messiah Priest. He knew what temptation was.

> *"For we do not have a high priest who is unable to empathize with our weaknesses, but we have one who has been tempted in every way, just as we are—yet he did not sin."* Hebrews 4:15

With this testing completed, Jesus was ready to set forth on his mission of preaching the good news of the kingdom of God and demonstrating the power of the kingdom in the miracles he would perform.

12-16. When he heard that Herod had arrested John the Baptist, Jesus returned to Galilee and, leaving Nazareth, went down to Capernaum by the Lake of Galilee in what had been the region of Zebulun and Naphtali. In that way the

words spoken by the prophet Isaiah were fulfilled: *"Land of Zebulun and land of Naphtali, lands beside the lake and beyond the Jordan River, Galilee, inhabited by people from the nations, those living in darkness, have seen a great light; upon those dwelling under a sentence of death, a light has risen."*[5]

Galilee was a place where Jews lived among people of other races: Canaanites, Greeks, and Romans. The crowds that followed Jesus must have included people of all these races. But that was prophetic. This message of the Kingdom of Heaven and of the Messiah King, though particularly directed to God's people the Jews, was a message for all people. It was a message for the world.

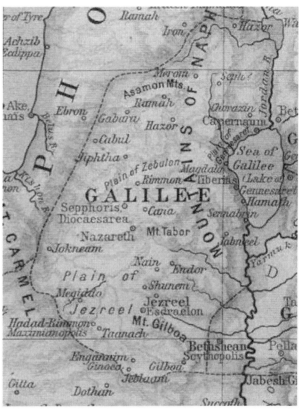

17. At that time Jesus began preaching. This was his message: "Repent, because the kingdom of heaven is close at hand."

Repentance means to turn from the way you are going and go God's way. We don't know how many responded to Jesus' message. But we do know that Peter and his brother Andrew and James and his brother John did. And their response to the message illustrates dramatically what repentance means.

18-22. As Jesus was walking by the Lake of Galilee, he came upon two brothers casting their net into the lake for they were fishermen. One was Simon (who is called Peter) and the other Andrew. Jesus said to them, "Follow me, and I will give you the job of fishing for men." And they immediately left their nets and followed him. A little

further along Jesus saw two other brothers, James and John, the sons of Zebedee, who along with their father were mending their nets. He called the brothers to follow him, and they immediately left their boat and their father and followed Jesus.

Repentance may mean something different for each one. God's purpose for Peter and Andrew will probably not be exactly God's purpose for us. But repentance does mean leaving and following. And we must ask ourselves if we have truly left our way and are truly following Jesus.

23-25. Then Jesus went through Galilee, teaching in the synagogues. As he made known the good news of the kingdom of God and healed every disease and disorder among the people, his fame spread far and wide even throughout Syria, and people brought to him those who were sick and afflicted with various diseases and pains and those controlled by demons, as well as epileptics and paralytics. And Jesus healed them. Great crowds were following him, people from Galilee and Decapolis and from Jerusalem and Judea and from the east side of the Jordan River.

Thus began Jesus' life of teaching and healing. It would only be three years. But in that time the world was turned on its head, and history took a new course.

Galilee was the place Jesus chose to start.

Footnotes

1. Deuteronomy 8:3. This verse tells us that we live by God's provision. Jesus was declaring his dependence upon the Father, not upon his own power.

2. Psalm 91:11,12.

3. Deuteronomy 6:16.

4. Deuteronomy 6:13.

5. Isaiah 9:1,2. This is the first part of a chapter that clearly spoke of the Messiah. Jesus chose to live in Capernaum and preach in the region of Galilee that he might fulfill these words of Isaiah.

Chapter 5

Kingdom Character

An etching by Jan Luyken from the Phillip Medhurst Collection of Bible illustrations, 18th century

If you step back a little and look at the things Jesus taught, they are radical. Nowhere is this seen more clearly than in the Sermon on the Mount in Matthew chapters five through seven. They are so radical that some have called the kingdom Jesus describes the "upside down kingdom" because every attitude and behavior recommended to the citizens of this kingdom is contrary to the culture of the world we live in and to the inclination of our natures.

In the next three chapters the Messiah Jesus describes the new kingdom of which he is King.

1-3. When Jesus saw the crowds that had followed him, he climbed a hill and sat down with his followers next to him, and he began to teach them. He said, "Those who know they are spiritually needy will have real joy, for they truly belong to God's kingdom."

Jesus began by describing the character a citizen in the upside down kingdom would have. The first character trait is being "poor in spirit," which is another way of saying humble. Such a person recognizes deeply his spiritual need.

Those who belong to the kingdom of this world would say the world doesn't work that way. Don't let anyone see you as needy. Neediness is weakness, and they'll walk all over you. But Jesus said those who recognize their need and look to God and his grace are the happy ones. They belong to the upside down kingdom.

4. "Those who are filled with sadness over sin will have real joy, for God himself will comfort them with the promise of his pardon."

The two characteristics of sadness and joy seemed mutually exclusive. But they are not. Only as we come to the Lord with sadness over sin, ours and others', can we experience his forgiveness and the joy of seeing others forgiven.

Jesus continued,

5. "Those who put others before themselves will have real joy, for they will gain the world God has promised to his people."

That must have seemed a crazy idea to those who were obsessed about building their own little kingdoms with themselves as king. Putting others before yourself will get you nowhere. But in the end, all the kingdoms we build come tumbling down, and we have gained nothing. But lifting others up? That is a joy both now and forever.

6. "Those who have a deep longing to see the right prevail will have real joy, for they will see their longings satisfied."

The attitudes that characterize the citizens of the kingdom of God will always result in action. The kingdom citizen will promote others and give away his good for the sake of others, for that is his - or her - deepest longing. It is his character. He will work for the protection of those in danger and for justice for the helpless. It will happen. In ways small and great, righteousness (doing right) will overcome injustice. And ultimately, when this age has come to an end and the next begins, righteousness will reign from that time until forever.

7. "Those who show kindness and mercy will have real joy, for they will enjoy God's mercy."

It is God's character to be merciful by showing kindness to those who don't deserve it or to those who desperately need it. And it is his joy to do so. And that character is infused into the citizens of his kingdom. They too find great joy in showing kindness.

8. "Those whose hearts are pure and unencumbered by evil will have real joy, for they have the privilege of knowing God as his children."

The heart encumbered by evil, the heart focused on evil or overwhelmed by evil, is in turmoil. It has no peace. The heart free of all that and focused on God is satisfied and at peace with God, as a child is at peace in the arms of her mother.

9. Those who work for peace will have real joy, for they will be known as God's children."

Working for peace is hard work. Nevertheless, joy will come, for some will embrace peace and find in it God's peace. That is the experience of those who give their lives to work in hard places to bring hope and peace to the hopeless. People who go and work with Samaritan's Purse or World Relief or with their local church to make life better for those who are experiencing the turmoil of war and economic calamity always come home saying this was the best experience of their lives. It was a time of great joy.

Jesus continued,

10. "Those who are mistreated because they do right will have real joy, for they will enjoy the kingdom of heaven."

There is no promise that following the Messiah King will exempt anyone from pain or hardship. In fact, it almost guarantees he will experience difficulty, just as Jesus experienced opposition from those who chose violence over peace. But there is coming a day when the Kingdom of Heaven will prevail, and evil will perish. Live for that day. Endure the harsh treatment you may experience now for righteousness because in that day the blessing of the kingdom will sweep away every memory of pain. Live with eternity in view.

11-12. "When people hate you and mistreat you and falsely accuse you of all kinds of evil just because you belong to me, rejoice. Yes, be glad, for this is what people did to the prophets who lived before you."

The prophets suffered insult and gave their lives for something that was far off, something they would not see in their lifetimes but saw in their minds and spirits. They chose to identify themselves with that Kingdom rather than with the kingdom of this world. They suffered for the Kingdom that was to come. And God's Kingdom will come. When it comes in its fullness, the insults they suffered or which we may suffer will be small in comparison with the glory of that kingdom.

13. "You of whom these things are true, you are the salt that preserves this world. (But take care. If salt loses its taste, it is of no value. It is of no more value than sand. It will be thrown out and walked on like dirt.)

14-16. "You of whom these things are true are the light that illuminates this dark world. Just as a city on a hill cannot be hidden, your light will provide light for all. Men do not hide a lamp under a basket. No, they put it out where it can give light to the entire house. In the same way let your good lives shine before all. Let them see how you live that they may give honor to God, your Father in heaven."

Those who belong to the Kingdom of Heaven and who have been transformed in their attitudes and characters are evidence that humility and purity and the genuine longing for peace and righteousness are good. It is God's purpose that they be so. That is why God leaves us here. By our transformed lives and characters, others will see God's goodness and give honor to him who transforms us.

Jesus then turned to a question that many of the religious Jews had, the Law.

17-20. "Don't think I have come to do away with the Law and the Prophets.[1] Rather I have come to fulfill them. I am serious[2], as long as the world continues, not the smallest letter will be deleted from the Law until all it speaks of is completed."

A big question for every Jew, and those were the readers to whom Matthew wrote his gospel, would be about the Law of God. To Jews, the Law was the most important thing God had given to his people. It was their greatest blessing. It was the thing that set them apart as God's people. What did Jesus have to say about the Law? They had heard that Jesus did away with the Law. They wanted to know.

It is a question Christians today have as well. We sometimes hear that the Law has been replaced by grace. We usually mean by that that God will overlook our failures to keep the Law and perhaps does not care about whether we pay attention to the Law. But that is wrong. In what follows, Jesus not only affirmed the rightness of the Law but went beyond to say that the purpose of the Law is deeper than mere outward and minimal obedience but goes to the obedience of the heart. It is there that the "religious" people of Jesus day failed. Though they strictly observed the letter of the Law, they failed to live the spirit of the Law.

"It follows then," Jesus continues, "that whoever ignores these commands and teaches others to ignore them will be the least in the kingdom of heaven. I am speaking the truth to you: Unless you live with greater attention to God's commands than the legal experts and religious leaders from the sect of the Pharisees, you will not enter the kingdom of God."

Jesus began with some examples of the difference between observing the letter of the Law and observing the spirit of the Law. Everyone knows murder is wrong. The religious leaders would have agreed. The letter of the law would be "do not murder." But in the upside down kingdom being angry with another person is equally wrong. Love - or the avoidance of anger - would be obeying the spirit of the law.

21-26. "For example, you know it has long been a command in the Law, 'Don't commit murder,' and all who commit murder will be in danger of the penalty required by the Law. But I tell, you whoever is angry with his brother or sister is in danger of judgment. If he says to a brother or sister, 'You scum bag,' he will be in danger of being found

guilty by the judges. But [I say] if he even so much as says, 'You fool,'[3] he will be in danger of being thrown into hell. Keeping good relationships with others is so important that if your brother or sister has something against you, you should put worship on hold and go to the one who has a complaint against you and make it right. Then you can worship with a clear conscience. I say to you again, make things right with anyone who holds anything against you. Do it before it gets to the point of his making a formal complaint. If you don't, you will find yourself in court, and the judge will find you guilty, and you will be thrown into prison. Seriously, if that happens, you will have to pay the full penalty for your crime."

Much of the law is about relationships between people. When the Law was broken and someone committed murder, for example, the Law required a penalty. However, many were following the rules - they were not murdering each other - but were failing to heal the broken relationships that led to breaking the Law. Jesus was simply saying that we must pay attention to the intent of the law, not the mere rules. The intent of the Law is good relationships. Make sure you do whatever is necessary to heal broken relationships. Do this whether you are the cause of the break or whether the other person is.

Then Jesus addressed another controversial topic, sexual faithfulness.

Adultery is wrong, almost everyone in Jesus' day would agree. But in the upside down kingdom even sexually desiring a person who is not your husband or wife is wrong.

27-30. "Again, you know that the Law says, 'Don't commit adultery,' but believe me when I tell you that everyone who looks at a married woman, [4] desiring her, has already committed adultery in his heart. This is so serious that you should tear out your eye and throw it away if it causes you to sin. It is better to lose an eye rather than suffer hell. Yes, if your hand causes you to sin, get rid of it. Throw it away. It is better to lose a hand than to suffer in hell."

This sounds extreme. And Jesus meant it to be. Of course, tearing out an eye or cutting off a hand does nothing to stem the course of lustful desire. The point Jesus was making is that sin, even sin hidden in the heart, is serious.

31-32. "Regarding divorce, the instructions were, 'whoever divorces his wife must give her a certificate that makes the divorce legal.' But I tell you that any divorce except for sexual unfaithfulness makes her an adulterer if she remarries. And if you marry a divorced woman, even if it is a legal divorce, you commit adultery with her."

Jesus will have more to say on this subject later, but here it is clear that divorce seriously violates God's purpose for our lives.

Jesus goes on. He addressed another issue, the swearing of oaths. The practice of sealing a promise with an oath had become too casual and too prevalent.

33-37. "Regarding oaths, it was written to our ancestors, 'Don't make a promise sealed by an oath you don't intend to keep; do what you have promised before the Lord.' But I tell you, don't swear any oath to seal a promise. Don't swear by heaven. That dishonors God. Don't swear an oath by the earth. The earth belongs to God, and such an oath makes God no more than a pawn in your game. Don't say, 'I swear by Jerusalem.' Jerusalem is the city of the Lord our King; you have no right to pledge it. Don't swear an oath pledging your head to seal a promise because you have no control over even your head.

"Simply mean what you say. If you say yes, keep that promise. If you say no, keep that promise. Anything beyond that is playing games with the truth and comes from the devil."

Just speak the truth. If you have a reputation for speaking the truth, people will accept your word, and there will be no need to resort to the childish practice of "cross my heart and hope to die" when you want people to really take your word seriously.

The next question was justice. It had become common for people to retaliate when they were injured. In fact, it was expected in the culture. It seemed just. But such retaliation reveals a heart defect.

38-42. "The Law required an eye for an eye and a tooth for a tooth. But I tell you, don't retaliate if someone hurts you.

In fact, if he hits you on your right cheek, turn the other to him as well. If he wants to take you to court and take your shirt, let him have your coat too. When he forces you to carry his burden one mile, go two. Give to the man who asks, and don't refuse a loan."

Jesus goes deeper than mere law keeping. In the upside down kingdom not only does one not hit back, he loves his enemies. God wants far more for us than superficial law keeping. He is interested in the heart attitudes that motivate our actions.

43-48. "The experts in the Law will tell you that it is written, 'You must love your neighbor,' and then they'll add, 'hate your enemies.'[5] But I tell you, love your enemies. Yes, and pray for the good of those who torment you. When you do, you will be acting like your Father in heaven, for he causes the sun to shine upon both the evil and the good and sends refreshing rain upon both the one who does right and the one who does wrong. If you only love those who love you, what's the big deal? Even thieves do that. And if you open your home to your brothers and sisters, what's so great about that? Even those with no respect for God do that. But do as your heavenly Father; love everyone. Then you will be a true and mature son."

Again and again Jesus said, "but I tell you." He was declaring his authority to interpret and explain the Law that God gave. Prophets would apply the Law to the lives of the people they spoke to, but this is different. Jesus' words claim for himself the very authority that God had in giving the Law. Only the Messiah had that authority.

Footnotes

1. The term *the Law and the Prophets* stood for the entire Hebrews S

2. Literally this expression is *truly, truly*. It is an expression common to the H language called a Hebraism. Jesus' words in the Gospel of Matthew and the gospels are full of these kinds of Hebrew idioms. It is evidence that Jesus sp Hebrew and that his words are faithfully captured by the gospel writers

3. The suggestion is that "scum bag" (*raka)* is the stronger insult, while "fool" is a milder. Jesus' point is that God holds us to a higher standard than human courts. Even a mild expression of contempt toward another person violates God's desire that we keep good relationships with others.

4. Both the context indicating that the sin was adultery (*moicheia*) and the word used for woman suggest it is a married woman. The word for woman (*gynaika*) in each of the fifty-three occurrences in the New Testament always indicates a married woman. If it were an unmarried woman the sin would have been sexual immorality (*porneias*). But that might be splitting hairs. Both adultery and sex outside of marriage are prohibited in the Bible.

5. There is no command in the Bible to hate your enemies. The teachers of the Law and the Pharisees added that idea and by that addition completely distorted God's intention.

criptures.
ebrew
ther
oke

Chapter 6

Kingdom Living

The Lord's Prayer by James Tissot, 1894
Brooklyn Museum, via Wikimedia

The Messiah king continued describing the culture of the new upside down kingdom. His point, It is not about you. It is about God and others.

> **1. "Don't make a big deal out of what you do for others or your acts of caring or charity. Don't do those things to be noticed. If you do you'll lose whatever reward you might have received from God.**

> **2-4. "So, when you give to someone in need, don't blow your horn. That's what the religious play actors do in their gatherings and in the streets. They want to be praised. But I tell you, the praise of men is all the praise they're going to get. You men and women of the Kingdom, when you give to those in need, don't even let your left hand know what your right hand is doing. What I'm saying is do your giving in secret. Your Father sees the secret things and will reward you."**

If giving is really about the person in need, then don't use your generosity as an occasion to call attention to yourself.

> **5-6. "And when you pray, don't be like the frauds who love to stand in the gathering places and in the streets and pray so they will be seen. They have their reward, such as it is. When you pray, find a secret place. Shut the door so no one will see or hear you, and pray to your Father. He knows what you say in secret. He sees, and you will receive what you ask."**

Jesus was not saying don't pray in public. We have many examples of public praying in the Bible. He was using an exaggeration to make his point. His point was don't pray in public to impress people. Here's a good principle: don't pray in public if you are not praying in private.

> **7-8. "And don't try to impress God with a lot of words. That's what people do who don't understand God. They think they'll get God's attention by mere empty repetition. Don't do that. You don't have to. Your Father knows what you need, even before you ask."**

Prayer is a conversation, not an incantation. It is not magic. Neither is it a means of twisting God's arm to get him to do what you want. Prayer requires that we get alone with God and listen. Then we will be able to ask for the thing God wants for us. And when we ask for what God wants, we'll certainly receive it.

Prayer does change things. But remember, the thing most needing change is you.

9-13. "So, when you pray, pray like this:

Heavenly Father, may you be famous for your holiness. May your kingdom come and your purposes be done here and now on earth, even as they are always done in heaven. Give us the food we need day by day, and forgive us when we fail, in the same way we forgive those who fail us. And don't let us be caught up in temptation, but save us from all that is evil."

This prayer is a model for praying; it is not a prayer to be prayed by rote or as a routine. Real prayer is not routine, even the prayer we may say at a meal should not be routine. It should always be genuine. Of course, we can pray these words Jesus gave us genuinely, and when we pray them, even when we pray them together as part of a group worship time, they should be genuine.

14-15. "If you forgive others when they fail you, your Father will also forgive you. But if you withhold forgiveness from others, your Father in heaven will withhold forgiveness from you, as well."

This is not a condition of forgiveness. It is a test of the heart. Are we truly aligned with God's heart? Then we will forgive. And as we are aligned with God, we will be in position to be forgiven, for we understand our need, and confessing that need, are forgiven.

16-17. "Now, about fasting: When you fast and go without food for a time in devotion to God, don't be a play actor and do it with sad faces so that others will think you super-religious. The praise those hypocrites get from men is all they're going to get. When you fast, however, clean up and look normal. That way no one will see your devotion except your Father. He knows the secret things and will satisfy your longings."

Fasting had become a ritual duty for the Jews, and the point of fasting had been lost. The point is that fasting allows you to focus your spiritual, emotional, and physical energy upon God and upon the need for which you may be praying, whether that is a personal spiritual need or the need of someone else.

Telling other people that you are fasting and making a big deal about it may make you look spiritual, but it makes the fasting no more than an outward show.

19-21. "Neither should you collect a lot of stuff. The moths will eat holes in it. Or it will rust like a wrecked car out in the rain. Or it will be stolen, and you'll lose it all. Rather, put your valuables in heaven where there are neither moths nor rust nor thieves to break in and steal. Here's the principle: Your heart will be where your valuables are – either in heaven or wrapped up with all this stuff around you."

When it comes to money and stuff, the culture of this world tells us to get as much as we can. But in the upside down kingdom, money and material things are unimportant. It is serving God that is important.

22-23. "Consider. Your eyes are the entrance of light. If your eyes are healthy, you'll see clearly and be able to get around unhindered. But if your eyes don't see, you'll stumble. Now, if the light you think you have is actually darkness, that will be darkness for sure."

If you don't judge by God's standards but by man's, you will never be able to judge the true value of things or their rightness or goodness; you will be like a blind man who can't see where he is going but who thinks he does. No matter how careful you are you will never end up where God wants you to be. For example, if you think that owning things is important, you will end up justifying whatever means are needed to gain things. You will treat things as more important than people. But that is the opposite of what Jesus said. Remember, it is not about you but about others and God.

Jesus was speaking directly to the religious leaders of his day, for this is exactly what they were doing. They were judging the rightness or goodness of things based on the superficial and outward appearance of right and good; their eyes didn't see clearly. They were like blind men trying to feel their way through life thinking they could see. They could never achieve true goodness by doing that. The best they could do was to appear to be good.

God begins deeper, at the level of the heart. That is where the truth about us lies. If we are to be truly good, then our heart must be good first.

24. "Remember, you can't be committed to two leaders. You will find yourself torn between whom to follow. Which will it be? You'll end up choosing one over the other. So, when it comes to money and God, you can't make both of them gods.

25-26. "Here's the bottom line. Don't obsess about what you're going to eat or drink or about clothes. Life is about more than that. Look at the birds flying over your heads. They don't plant crops, reap a harvest, or put it away in barns, yet your heavenly Father feeds them. Don't you think you mean more to him than the birds?"

Jesus was not telling people not to prepare for the future. That would not agree with what the Bible says. The book of Proverbs, for example, tells us it is prudent to save for the future. Jesus was simply making a point by using an exaggerated example. His point was that we should not be worried or anxious about the future. We don't have to pile up more and more stuff just in case. No, don't be anxious. God takes care of us.

27-30. "Or how much can worry do to lengthen your life? Can you add a single hour to it by worry? Or how about clothing? Why be obsessed? Look at the lilies in the fields. They grow without working or worrying about what they will wear. But look again, even Solomon decked out in his best did not have clothes as beautiful as these flowers. So, if God clothes the lilies and the grasses, which live for only a day before they are used for fuel, don't you think he will care for you? How little faith you have!

31-33. "So, don't be anxious. Don't be obsessed about what you are going to eat or drink or what you will wear. That's what people do who don't know God. You should know that your heavenly Father knows you need these things. Leave it to him, and make it your goal to be a son or daughter of the Kingdom of God. Do what he desires, and he'll take care of all the rest.

34. "Live by this principle: Don't worry about tomorrow; there will be time tomorrow to deal with the problems of that day. Each day has enough for you to attend to all by itself."

The key word in each of these is *worry*. There is wonderful peace in relying on God's care for us. If we do, we will not be excessively buying more and more stuff. We will free up our money to use it to bless others and for God. And we will find that we are wonderfully satisfied with the things God does provide for us.

Chapter 7

Kingdom Living, cont'd

The Sermon on the Mount. Stained glass by Louis Comfort Tiffany in the Arlington Street Church, Boston. Photographed by John Stephen Dwyer. Via Wikimedia.

As Jesus came to the end of this comparison of the two kingdoms, he said something that is very important. He said there are only two ways of living. Either you belong to the kingdom of this world and live according to that culture, or you belong to the upside down kingdom and live according to that culture. You must choose.

One contrast between the two kingdoms is between judging others and looking soberly at your own faults.

1-2. "Don't be quick to condemn others because if you do, they will find just as much reason to condemn you; you'll be measured by the same standard."

Listen in on a few conversations at school or work. Most are about people not present, and most are not complimentary. We like to find fault in others. But in the upside down kingdom, we are not to condemn others. We are to remember we are not without fault ourselves.

It is better to do something about our own faults and sins than to be critical of others

3-5. "It is foolish to find fault with some small thing in a brother while ignoring a far greater fault in yourself. It is like saying to your brother, 'Let me take that speck out of your eye,' while you have a huge stick in your own eye. Don't be such a fraud. First take the stick out of your eye, then you will be able to see clearly to take the speck out of your brother's eye."

The truth is, we are most often critical of others because pointing out their failures makes us look good by comparison. That is what Jesus tells us to avoid.

However, if you read ahead a bit in the story, Jesus was very critical of the people who pushed themselves forward as religious leaders while at the same time they were far from living as God wanted. But Jesus could judge because he had no stick in his own eye; he was not trying to make himself look good by putting them down.

We, on the other hand, seldom are free from fault ourselves, and we call some things great faults or sins in others while we overlook other sins just as great in ourselves. And we often are critical just because we want to make ourselves look good by putting others down.

One of the current hot buttons for Christians is homosexuality. We are inclined to speak strongly about how homosexual sex is sin - and it is - yet we ignore things like divorce and sex outside marriage or pornography and act as though they are relatively small things, when the Bible actually speaks far more often about those things. We do not deal with this plank in our eyes, but are quick to pick at the speck in others' eyes. Jesus said don't do that.

It is necessary to call sin sin. We cannot avoid that. But be careful. Be sure, first, you have been straight with God about your own faults and sin. It will humble you. Then you are in a position to help others without judging them.

6. "Here's a proverb for you: Don't give dogs what is sacred or throw your pearls to the pigs. If you do, they might just stomp them into the mud or turn on you and attack."

Taken by itself, this proverb means don't talk about these things that are important to you with people who don't care; they will only trash your ideas. But taken in the context of what Jesus has been saying, he probably meant more specifically don't expect that others adopt these upside down kingdom principles if they don't have a heart that is toward God. It will seem like they are just a set of rules that don't make sense; they will think them foolish and throw them back in your face.

These Kingdoms principles are not rules we must live by. They picture what a Kingdom citizen will be like as he or she follows Jesus our Messiah King.

7-8. "Here's another proverb: Ask for what you need. It will be given. Seek for the thing you desire. You'll find it. Knock on the door. It will be opened. The fact is, everyone who asks receives what he needs; and the one who seeks finds what he is looking for; and to the one who knocks, the door is opened.

9-11. "Tell me. If your son asks for food, do you give him a rock? If he asks for fish, do you give him a snake? If you care enough for your son to give him the good things he needs, even though you are less than perfect, don't you think your Father in heaven will give you the good things you need when you ask?"

Coming to the end of the teaching about the Kingdom, Jesus encouraged his listeners to push on to know God more deeply and to receive from him all that he desires to give. Jesus could not in one message download into his hearers everything they needed to know or every truth they would ever need. And he could not by a simple sermon make them wise and strong in their relationship with God. But he did assure them that if they kept on asking and seeking and knocking they would find wisdom for living and fellowship with God. Those, after all, are the things they most needed. And they are the things God wanted for them. They are the things he wants for us. He will not hide them from us, especially if we keep pressing on to receive them from him.

12. "Here's a basic principle: Do to others the thing that you would like them to do to you. This sums up all that the Scriptures have to say about relationships."

This principle has been called The Golden Rule. It is a proverb and was not unique to Jesus. But it did capture the basic idea of this message called The Sermon on the Mount: it is not about me but about God and others.

Jesus then went on to highlight how critical it is to live as a citizen of the upside down kingdom.

13-14. "Choose the right road in life. The road that leads to destruction is a four-lane highway; it is easy to find and easy to travel. Many choose that wide road. But the road that leads to life is a single lane, and only a few find it."

The result of living as this world tells you is destruction; it is destruction both now and forever. But the result of living the life of the upside down kingdom is LIFE. There are two roads. You are on one or the other. Choose the way that leads to life.

15-20. "Watch out for slick salesmen of religion. They sound good, but they're out to take you and your money. You can tell them by how they live. You don't get grapes from thorn bushes or peaches from thistles. Healthy fruit trees always produce healthy fruit, and unhealthy trees produce poor fruit. It is just a fact. Good trees have good fruit. Sick trees have rotten fruit. But here's the warning: Trees that don't produce good fruit are cut down and burned. So, as for those salesmen of religion, you'll know them by the fruit they produce."

Be careful who you listen to. Be careful who you follow. There are many slick salesmen of religion out there. They promise a lot and deliver little. They are into it for themselves. They want your money or your devotion. They want to be popular, powerful, or rich. They will not lead you closer to God.

21-23. "There are many who will use my name for their own purposes who aren't people of the Kingdom of Heaven. Only those who do my Father's will are true people of the Kingdom. On the day of judgment, there will be many who will claim, 'We've preached in your name, cast out evil spirits in your name, done miracles in your name.' Then I will say to them, 'I never knew you. Leave me, you lawbreakers!'"

Jesus was speaking directly of the Pharisees who claimed to be God's spokesmen but were not really. But this warning is a sobering one for everyone who claims to be a follower of Jesus. Am I a true citizen of the Kingdom of God? If so, I will show it by my humility and obedience to Jesus. I will not be using Jesus for my own gain; I will be serving him.

24-27. "Everyone who truly hears the things I've been saying and does them is a wise man who builds his house on a firm foundation. When the rains and floods come and the winds beat against his house, it will not collapse because it is built on rock. But everyone who hears these words and does not do them is foolish, a man who builds his house upon sand. When the rains and floods and winds come, his house will fall and be completely destroyed."

Wrapping up, Jesus repeated what he has been saying throughout: doing is the point, doing from a true heart. Listening has little value if there is no doing.

28-29. When Jesus had finished teaching, the crowds who had followed him and had listened to all these words were amazed. His teaching was like nothing they had heard before; he taught with authority, unlike their rabbis and their experts in the Scriptures.

The Sermon on the Mount is the manifesto [1] of the kingdom. It is a prescription for living here and now - for those who have chosen the narrow path. And it is a description of the future. This is what heaven will be like.

FOOTNOTES

1. A manifesto is a public declaration of the values, goals, and methods of a person or group. In this case, The Sermon on the Mount was Jesus' public statement of what his Kingdom was like.

Chapter 8
The Authority of the King

Study for *Jesus in Capernaum* by Rodolpho Amoedo, 1885

In Biblical times Capernaum was one of the main trading villages in the Gennesaret area which was a vibrant populated and prosperous part of Palestine and was inhabited by about 1,500 people many of whom were fishermen. [The disciples Peter, Andrew, James, and John lived here.] Many travelers, caravans and traders passed through Capernaum on the Via Maris, the main trade route connecting Damascus in the north and Egypt in the south. There remains a Via Maris highway mile stone in Capernaum today.

From touristIsrael.com

Matthew has been showing his readers that the Messiah Jesus is the king of an upside down kingdom. Now in chapters eight and nine Matthew will show us the authority of the King.

1-4. When Jesus was finished teaching, he came down from the mountain, and the crowds followed him. Almost immediately a man with a skin disease called leprosy [1] met them. He knelt down before Jesus and said, "Master, if it is your desire, you could make me clean."

Chapter eight opens with Jesus healing a man who had a serious skin disease called leprosy. The interesting part of the story is that the question was not so much the power of the King to heal but whether it was his desire to heal. Jesus' replied that he did want to heal him.

This was not simply a random statement. It was intentionally chosen by Matthew for the purpose of showing his Jewish readers (and us) that the Messiah is for us. He is on our side, just as he was for this man. But the Messiah King is not merely *for us*. He is able to do something, and he did in this case. He healed the man.

And Jesus reached out and touched him saying, "It is my desire. Be clean." Immediately the leprosy was gone. Then Jesus told him, "Don't talk about this. But go to the priest and offer the sacrifice Moses instructed. It will be a proof to them you are clean."

In the next story a Roman military commander came to Jesus asking that Jesus heal his servant. When Jesus told him he would come with him to heal the servant, the Roman told Jesus that he only needed to say the word and his servant would be healed. Jesus marveled at this man's faith, and he gave the command that the servant be healed.

5-13. Now, when they reached Capernaum, a Roman centurion[2] found Jesus and appealed to him, "Master, my servant is lying paralyzed in my home and is in agony."

Jesus responded to him, "I will come with you and heal him."

But the centurion replied, "Master, I am unworthy to have you come to my home; only command, and my servant will be healed. For I am a man under authority and have

soldiers under me. I only have to command one of my men, 'go,' and he goes, or to command another 'come,' and he comes. And to my servant I only have to say, 'Do this,' and he does it."

When Jesus heard this, he was impressed, saying to those who were following him, "I have not seen this kind of faith even among the people of Israel, who know well God's power. I tell you that many will come from the nations in the east and in the west to sit at the banquet with Abraham, Isaac, and Jacob in the Kingdom of Heaven; while those who are Israelites will suffer the darkness of hell. In that place there will be terrible sorrow and grief."

Then Jesus said to the centurion, "Go. It will be done as you have asked and believed." And the man's servant was healed even as Jesus spoke.

The point of these stories is that it requires faith in Jesus the Messiah King to be a citizen of the upside down kingdom and to enjoy his care. That does not mean that you simply have to believe that Jesus is the Messiah. It means that you must place yourself under the King in the same way that the centurion placed himself under Jesus' authority. You must trust him as your King and act on that trust.

In verses 14 through 17 Matthew told his readers that Jesus healed not only those who were ill, but he also healed those under the control of evil spirits called demons. Then Matthew added that these things showed that Jesus was truly the Messiah because he fulfilled the prediction of the Old Testament prophet Isaiah.

14-17. When Jesus reached Peter's house and entered, he saw Peter's mother-in-law sick with a fever and lying on her bed. When he touched her hand, the fever left her, and she rose from the bed and began to serve as was customary for a hostess. When evening came, the people of Capernaum and the surrounding countryside brought many who were controlled by evil spirits to Jesus, and he ordered the spirits to leave and healed everyone who was sick. This fulfilled what the prophet Isaiah had written about Messiah: *"He took away our illnesses and carried our diseases."*

After such displays of power and care for people, you would think that everyone would want to be a follower of Jesus and a citizen of his Kingdom. And in fact, several men did come to Jesus wanting to be disciples in the Kingdom. Surprisingly, Jesus did not encourage them. He told one man that being a follower would mean hardship and that he should think it over before volunteering. Being a follower of Jesus and a citizen of the Kingdom of Heaven is a serious thing.

18-22. Sometime later a crowd had again gathered around him, but when Jesus saw them he told his disciples to take him across the lake and away from the crowd. Before they left, a man who was an expert in the Hebrew Scriptures approached him and said, "Teacher, I will follow you."

Jesus replied, "Foxes have dens in which they live, and birds have nests, but the Son of Man [3] has no place to call home."

Jesus meant that literally; he had no permanent home. But he meant it in a figurative way as well. He did not belong to this world. And his reply to this would-be-disciple told him that anyone who chooses to follow must regard himself as homeless also, for that may well be the price of following.

Another who would be a disciple said to Jesus, "Master, let me return home until I have fulfilled my responsibilities to my father."

But Jesus said to him, "The time is now. Follow me. Leave it to those who have no concern for the urgency of the hour to stay at home and attend to the duties of home."

This man volunteered to be a disciple of Jesus, but he wanted to put it off until he had fulfilled the responsibilities he had toward his parent. But Jesus told him that becoming a follower could not be put off or delayed. He would have to make up his mind and either follow Jesus now or go home.

23-27. When Jesus had gotten into the boat, his disciples followed him. While they were upon the lake there suddenly arose a strong storm with winds driving the waves and threatening to swamp the boat. But Jesus was asleep.

The disciples, fearing that they were going to die in this storm, woke Jesus and said to him, "Save us, Master. We are going to drown."

And Jesus replied, "Why are you afraid? Do you have no faith?" He then stood and rebuked the wind and the waves, and immediately they were calm. The men were amazed. They said among themselves, "What kind of a man is this? Even the winds and waves obey him."

The point of these stories is that the Messiah King has incredible authority. He healed diseases. He cast out evil spirits. He commanded even the wind. Those things were impressive. This Messiah was the real deal.

But to be a member of his Kingdom requires serious commitment to Jesus as King. It is not like signing up on a website and expecting an email notice of a special offer now and then. Signing up to be a follower should be taken seriously. There will be hardship for all who choose to follow him. But there is also extraordinary benefit. Jesus can protect us in the most dangerous places, and he heals us - more deeply than just our physical diseases. He heals our soul.

28-34. When they arrived at the far shore of the lake, in the country of the Gadarenes, two men controlled by evil spirits came out from among the tombs and approached Jesus. They were so fierce that no one would dare to travel along that path anymore. They shouted loudly, "Why have you come here , O Son of God? Have you come to punish us before the appointed time?"

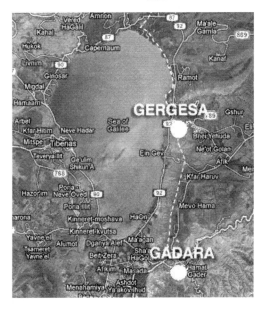

The place where Jesus cast out the evil spirits from the two men living among the tombs has long been identified as Gergesa. But that did not fit well with the known location of Gadara, which is the location indicated in the Bible. The problem was that Gadara was a long way from the lake of Galilee. Recent archaeological work, however, shows that the lake was once much higher, and that Gadara does fit the description in the Bible.

Now, there was a herd of pigs feeding some distance away. And the spirits who commanded these men begged saying, "If you are going to throw us out, send us away into the pigs."

And Jesus spoke simply. "Go." The evil spirits then came out of the men and went into the pigs, and the whole herd stampeded down the steep bank and into the lake and drowned.

The men herding the pigs ran. When they got back to town, they told what had happened, especially what had happened to the men with evil spirits. At that the whole town came out to where Jesus was. When they saw him they pleaded with him to leave their country.

Why did the people of Gadara ask Jesus to leave? Some have speculated that the people of Gadara, who were not Jews, depended upon raising pigs as the local industry. They saw the destruction of the pigs as a blow to their livelihood. Perhaps so.

But in the flow of the story what has been striking to people is the power of Jesus. So, it is likely that Matthew meant to underscore the fact that not everyone was comfortable with Jesus' power. It was out of their control. It threatened them. It threatened their comfortable way of life. The people of Gadara instinctively knew that to welcome Jesus would change their lives, and they didn't want to change.

For others these demonstrations of Jesus' power and his message drew them to him.

FOOTNOTES

1. Leprosy was a skin disease, but it probably was not the same as what we call leprosy today. In the Old Testament someone with leprosy was considered unclean. That meant anyone with leprosy was isolated from other people and could not take part in any religious gathering.

2. A Roman centurion was an officer in the Roman army. He commanded a group of 100 soldiers.

3. Jesus called himself "the Son of Man." Those words had a double meaning. They could mean simply that he identified himself as a man, as was everyone else. But it had another meaning. It could be connected with Daniel 7:13 where one like "a son of man" was led into the presence of God and was given authority and power and glory and whom all nations worshiped. It is likely Jesus meant it to be understood in both senses.

Chapter 9
The Authority of the King, cont'd

The Calling of Saint Matthew by-Caravaggo (1599-1600)
Matthew points to himself as if incredulous that Jesus would call him. The other tax collectors are preoccupied with counting their money.

You would think everyone would like a humble King who went around healing people. Jesus seemed to be no threat to anyone. But chapter nine tells us that not everyone thought that way. There is another kingdom, and that kingdom was not going away without a fight.

The first story in chapter nine is about the healing of a man who had been paralysed. But the problem was that Jesus not only healed the man, he forgave his sins.

1-8. Leaving the Gadarenes,[1] Jesus got into the boat and crossed back over the lake to his own city, Capernaum. When he arrived some people brought him a man, paralysed and lying on a bed. Seeing their faith Jesus said to the paralytic, "Be encouraged, my son, your sins are forgiven."

Who forgives sin? No one who heard these words, including Matthew's Jewish readers, would have gotten the answer wrong. Only God forgives sins. And that meant Jesus was making the astounding claim to be God - or to be acting as God's equal.

Some of the experts in Jewish law looking on said among themselves, "This man violates the Law. He claims to have the authority only God has."

But Jesus knew what they were thinking, and said, "Why do you judge me in your hearts? But tell me, which is easier to say: 'Your sins are forgiven,' or 'Get up and walk?'[2] But so you may understand that the Son of Man has the authority on earth to forgive sins" – he said this now to the paralytic – "Get up, take your litter and go home." And the man did so.

When the crowds saw and heard this they were afraid, and they gave glory to God for giving such authority to this man Jesus.

Most people would be sceptical about anyone who claimed to be God or to be speaking with the authority of God; they are usually crazy. But the things Jesus was doing pointed to an authority and power only God could have.

That was a problem for some people. There was, of course, the theological problem of a man being God's equal. But there was another problem. The experts in the Law and the Pharisees had become the authorities. They were the religious professionals. And they realized Jesus with his upside down kingdom would turn their lives upside down. He would expose their selfishness and the emptiness of their religion. In his upside down kingdom the power they had and the respect people had for them would be gone. They could not allow Jesus to replace them in the eyes of the people. They became his enemy.

They attacked Jesus. First, they told people that he could not be a good person because he implied the authority he had was the same as the authority God had. Then, they said that Jesus was evil and he was casting out evil spirits because Satan had given him that power.

Jesus did not reply to their accusations. He let his actions speak for him. He healed the sick, even a woman sick for many years whom no one could help. He opened the eyes of people who were blind. He even brought a dead girl back to life.

Not only so, he chose people the Pharisees considered worthless to be his followers. And that was a scandal to these religious men, and they despised him.

9-13. As Jesus travelled through the cities of Galilee, he saw a man called Matthew.[3] He was sitting at a booth where he worked collecting taxes. Jesus said to him, "Follow me." And Matthew left his tax booth and followed Jesus.

Later as Jesus and his disciples were eating dinner at Matthew's home, many of Matthew's friends among the tax collectors and other disreputable people came and joined them. When men of the Pharisees, the religious elite, saw this they questioned the disciples, "How is it that your so called teacher is eating with tax collectors and their friends?"

Jesus overheard what they were saying and replied, "The healthy do not need a doctor, but the sick do. But look in your Scriptures. Doesn't it say, 'I desire love,[4] and not sacrifice.' And that is why I've come – not to call those who think they are doing right, but to call back to God those who know they are failures."[5]

This was pretty tough talk. Jesus was saying that these men who considered themselves religious and superior to rabble like Matthew were themselves not following the Scriptures. You can imagine that they would not like what Jesus was saying, but they had a problem. What he was saying was true.

There were others who saw the problems with religion but who still were not sure how much change was necessary. They wanted to renew the practices and traditions of the Old Testament, not rewrite them. Some of these were disciples of John the Baptist.

14-17. After this some who were disciples of John the Baptist came and asked Jesus, "We and the religious leaders observe the prescribed fasts [6] but your disciples do not. Why?"

Jesus replied, "Do people going to a wedding with the groom sorrow? But there will come a day when the groom is taken from them. Then they will sorrow. But regarding fasting, a person does not patch an old shirt with a piece of new unshrunk cloth. If he does, when the shirt is washed, the new patch will shrink and tear a larger hole in the shirt than before."

Matthew's readers were Jews. One of the biggest questions they had when it came to following this Messiah was how much their religious practices and traditions would have to change: Is this a whole new thing? Or is this Messiah just correcting some of the failures that had crept into the Jewish faith?

"Neither do people put unfermented grape juice in old worn out wineskins. [7] If they do when the juice ferments the process will burst the wineskins and the wine will be lost. No, they put grape juice for fermentation in new skins that will stretch as the grape juice ferments and turns into wine."

Jesus explained that he was doing a new thing, that God was doing a new thing. And the new thing did not fit into the same old religious thinking or the rituals of the past. He used the metaphor of the new wine in old wine skins, but the way of doing things in the past is what he meant.

That, of course, did not make the Pharisees feel better about Jesus. They had become the rulers of the old religion. And they didn't want to give up their power or positions. They would become more and more the enemies of Jesus in the chapters that follow.

Jesus had healed diseases of all kinds. He had cast out demons. He had commanded the winds and the storm. Impressive! But then a man, a man of standing in the community, came to him with an impossible request: "Raise my daughter to life." And Jesus did.

18-26. While Jesus was speaking to these men, a man who was a well-known official of the city came and bowed before Jesus. "My daughter has died," he said. "Please come and put your hands on her that she may live." Immediately Jesus stood and followed the man, and his disciples with him.

"Immediately." Jesus was not interested in quibbling about trifles. Fasting, especially ritual fasting, was a trifle. Jesus was interested in people, so when there was a need, he chose action over words. He easily left the theological debate to live as the Father sent him to live - the life of God among men.

As they were on their way to the man's house, a woman who had suffered from bleeding for twelve years caught up with Jesus, unnoticed by either Jesus or the crowd, and touched just the fringe of his robe. She said to herself, "If I only touch his robe, I will be healed."

But Jesus, knowing what she had done, turned to her. "Be encouraged, dear daughter; your faith has made you well," he said. And at that moment she was healed.

Faith is not a magic pill. It is trust in a promise of God.

This woman knew that Jesus was the Messiah King, the Son of God. She knew he had healed others, many others; he was able. And she saw in Jesus a promise, the promise of compassion. And she acted in trust on that promise. Jesus only affirmed her trust: "Your faith has made you well."

Does faith heal today? There are those who say so. "If only you have faith, God will heal you," they say. "If you are not healed, it must be that you don't have enough faith." But that sort of faith is faith in faith, not faith in a promise of God. When God makes a specific promise to us, we may trust absolutely in his promise. God can heal. He does heal. But he may choose to carry us through the difficulties of illness and even death for his purpose rather than heal. Or he may choose to heal. If we ask and wait upon his answer, he will tell us what his will is, and if it is to heal, he certainly will. We can absolutely trust in his promise.

When they all finally arrived at the official's house and Jesus saw the commotion of the mourners and the flute players preparing for the girl's burial, he said, "Go away. The girl is not dead. She is only sleeping." But they laughed at this.

Then when the crowd had been sent outside, Jesus went in and took the girl by the hand, and she sat up. Alive! And the mourners, when they heard of it, were so astonished that the news of this went everywhere.

We should remember that Matthew wrote this gospel not so many years after these events that his readers could not have checked out these claims. This story was amazing. It circulated widely. Matthew was not telling his readers something new; he is just reminding them: Yes. Jesus did even this; he raised the dead. Such is the authority and power of this Messiah King.

27-31. As Jesus and his disciples were leaving that place, a man controlled by an evil spirit and unable to speak was brought to him. Jesus commanded the evil spirit to leave him, and when the spirit had left, the man was able to speak again. The crowds who followed Jesus were astonished. "We've never heard of anything like this in all Israel," they said. But the religious teachers argued with them, "He commands these spirits by the power of the prince of demons."

Was Jesus a wolf in sheep's clothing as his enemies claimed? No. He acted out of compassion not malice. His compassion and care for people was sufficient response to his accusers.

But this charge that Jesus was doing these things by the power of Satan was a charge that continued to be the response of Jesus' enemies for many years. Matthew's readers had almost certainly heard it. His enemies could not deny the miracles, so they tried to impugn the character of the miracle worker. He's Satan personified, they said. But their accusations did not fly. The crowds kept coming.

35-38. In these days Jesus went through all the cities and villages telling people everywhere the good news of the Kingdom and healing every illness and infirmity. He had compassion on the crowds that everywhere came to him. He saw them as troubled and helpless, like sheep without a

shepherd to care for them. And he said to his disciples, "The harvest is great, but there are few who work to bring it in. Ask the Lord, to whom this harvest belongs, to send out more workers to bring in the crops."

And Jesus' final words?

There are no chapter divisions in the original text of Matthew's Gospel. The first words of chapter ten should be read with the last words of chapter nine with no break: "Ask the Lord, to whom this harvest belongs, to send out more workers to bring in the crops ... and calling his twelve disciples he gave them power." When we read Matthew's words like that, it is clear that Jesus expected these twelve disciples to be harvesters. They will be the answer to their own prayers.

There is a caution here. Do not pray for harvesters unless you are serious, for God will certainly call you to be one of those harvesters....

FOOTNOTES

1. The chapter divisions are a later addition to the story and sometimes divide a narrative that should be seen as a single piece. That is the case here. Jesus immediately did as the Gadarenes requested.

2. Jesus had been doing miracles like this all along. They were evidence that he had the authority of God. And these men had seen it. That is why Jesus challenged them with his question.

3. Read much more about Matthew, who was not only a disciple but the author of this book, in the "Background" to Matthew at the end of this book.

4. Hosea 6, especially verse 6. Jesus refers to this passage in the Hebrew Scriptures, but he seems to quote the Septuagint Greek translation rather than the Hebrew. The Pharisees no doubt knew it well. It was a strong rebuke for those who were all about religious rules and ceremony but had no real love for God. The usual translation as *mercy* is faithful to the Greek of Matthew but misses the point of Hosea 6:6. There the word in Hebrew is *hesed* meaning loyal love.

5. Often there is a deeper meaning implied in Jesus' words. Literally he said, "I did not come to call the righteous, but sinners." The Pharisees considered themselves the righteous. But would they see that they are as equally in need of turning to God as these whom they contemptuously call "sinners?"

6. There were fasts that the Old Testament called for. But they had a purpose. They were days of sorrow for sin. However, according to **Zechariah 8:19**, in the day that God determines to do good to Jerusalem those fasts would be changed to celebrations of joy. That was what God was offering through Jesus, a day when God would do good to Jerusalem. Regular fasting was, therefore, one of the old things that were passing away.

7. Grape juice was stored in bottles made out of the skins of an animal while it fermented and turned to wine. That bottle was called a wineskin. The fermentation process causes a gas to be given off. If the grape juice was stored in a wineskin that stretched, as a new wineskin would, the gas would expand without harm. But if the wineskin had been used before, all the stretch was gone, and it would burst from the pressure of the gas.

Chapter 10
Building the Kingdom

Christ and the Apostles in Tiffany glass, 1890

Jesus began to gather together a few men who had embraced the message of the Kingdom of Heaven, the upside down kingdom. He knew what was in the future for him; he would die on a cross. And he knew that others would need to carry on his mission to tell people about God's love. They would be those who would extend his call to all people: "Return to God. He loves you. He desires to be your friend."

He chose twelve men. Their names are listed in chapter ten. Among them were common men like Peter and Andrew, brothers who were fishermen, and James and John, cousins of Jesus and also fishermen. (John would later write the Gospel of John.) There was one man who was a political radical from a group that wanted to take the land of the Jews back from the Romans by force if necessary, Simon the Zealot. Another was the man who wrote the book of Matthew, a tax collector. There was one man who became known as the doubter, Thomas. And there was also Judas Iscariot, the man who later would turn Jesus over to his enemies.

1-4. And Jesus called twelve disciples. He gave them authority to cast out evil spirits and to heal every disease and infirmity. The names of the twelve, who became known as apostles,[1] are these: The first is Simon, who was named Peter by Jesus, and then Andrew, Simon's brother. Next are the sons of Zebedee named James and John. Next there are Philip, Bartholomew and Thomas. Then there is Matthew, the tax collector. And then James the son of Alphaeus.[2] Then Thaddaeus and Simon, who was a Zealot. And then Judas Iscariot, the one who betrayed him.

None of these men were from the higher class, and they were mostly uneducated by the standards of the Greeks and Romans. But in the next thirty years they would take the message of Jesus to the farthest places in the Roman Empire. They would travel as far west as Spain and as far east as India. In every place they would find people who, when they heard about Jesus, wanted to follow him and be a part of his kingdom.

But that happens later. At this point in the story, the disciples were still learning.

5-15. Jesus sent these twelve disciples out to preach the good news about the Kingdom. His instructions were: "Go to the lost sheep of Israel, not to non-Jews or Samaritans. Preach that the Kingdom of Heaven is close at hand. Heal the sick, raise the dead to life, cleanse those with leprosy,

and cast out demons. You received the gift of life without paying anything for it, so do these good things without asking payment."

Part of their preparation was to do what Jesus had been doing. They were to go out in groups of two to all the towns and villages of the Jews and tell the people that the Kingdom of God had begun and that they could be a part of it.

They began telling the message to the Jews. Including that note about their first objective being the Jews was important to Matthew's purpose. God had a special place in his heart for the Jews, and Matthew wanted his readers to understand that had not changed. The message that is the good news of God's Kingdom would be for everyone, but it was especially for the Jews.

"But don't take money with you. Don't pack a bag or take extra clothes or shoes or an extra walking stick. The worker is worthy of payment. So in whatever town or village you enter, find someone who respects and honours the message you bring. Stay with him for as long as you remain in the village."[3]

"As you enter his house honor it and the hospitality of your host. If your host is a worthy man, speak a blessing of peace upon the home. But if he turns out to be undeserving or disrespectful, warn him. And if any refuse to receive you or listen to your message, leave them to their choice with this warning: It will be better for the evil cities of Sodom and Gomorrah on the day of judgment than for this place."

Jesus did not soften the consequences that would follow to those who did not receive these messengers or their message. It would be equal to God's judgment that had rained down on the infamous cities of Sodom and Gomorrah. That would have caused Matthew's readers pause. What they would do with the message and with the Messiah Jesus had serious implications.

It has serious implications for us today.

16-20. "Understand, I am sending you to be sheep surrounded by wolves. So be as cautious as snakes and as harmless as doves. Yes, I tell you, be prepared. You will be accused as criminals, and you'll be beaten up in the religious gatherings. You will be tried as rebels before

governors and kings because you are my followers. But this will be your chance to tell these rulers and unbelievers about me."

Jesus told them they should expect opposition. There would be some people who would hate them. But Jesus said they were to be like sheep among wolves. They were not to defend themselves. If they were arrested and taken before the court, they were to simply say what the Spirit of God gave them to say.

Jesus warns us to expect opposition as well but to push through it to declare his love and offer of forgiveness. It is the only hope for this world.

"When you are arrested, don't worry about putting together a defence. God will give you the words when you have a chance to speak. It will not be you but the Spirit of your Father speaking through you.

21-23. "There will come a time when a brother will turn his brother over to the authorities and a father his own child, and children will turn their parents over to the executioner. All will hate you because you are my followers. But endure to the end and you will be saved. When you are harassed in one town, go on to the next. I promise you, the task is so great that the Son of Man will return before you have preached in all the towns of Israel."

Although these instructions and warnings were specific to the twelve disciples they can be applied to anyone who is a follower of the Messiah, then and now. However, in a particular way, they could be applied personally by every Jewish reader of this book.

The first readers of Matthew's gospel were experiencing these very things. The Jewish nation was turning away from this small group that had been called "The Way." The nation and its leaders had rejected their Messiah. They had persecuted the followers of Jesus. And they were about to be scattered and their holy city destroyed by the Romans. From that point on there would be a deep hostility between Jews and the followers of the Messiah Jesus, as there remains today. Yet, Jesus was saying to the Jews who had believed in him to keep on telling the message to their people. "Keep on. You will not complete that task before the Son of Man returns."

Today there are many Messianic Jews. These are Jews who believe in Jesus as their Messiah. And many of them are focused on telling their fellow Jews this message of God's love and of wholeness and salvation through Jesus. They often encounter opposition, but they are also seeing many come to the Savior.

24-25. "Students should not expect better than their teacher, or servants than their master. Students should make it their aim to be like their teacher and servants like their master. If I, the master of the household, am called the chief of demons, my servants will not be treated any better.

26-33. "But don't be afraid of them. Stay at your job. Remember the proverb: 'Nothing is covered that will not be uncovered, and nothing is hidden that will not be known.' That is what you are doing; you are uncovering. What I tell you privately, announce publicly; what you hear whispered shout from the housetops. Don't be afraid of your enemies who can only kill the body but cannot touch the soul. Rather fear the one who can destroy both the body and soul in hell."

In the years that followed, almost every one of these twelve men went on to take the message of the Kingdom of God to Jews (and to non-Jews) scattered around the Roman Empire. Almost all of them died as martyrs because they refused to be afraid of their enemies. They believed that it was far more important to speak God's message of salvation than to hide the truth.

Since the first century millions more have followed in their footsteps, believing as they did: The worst that men can do is kill you. Respect God, for he holds your eternity in his hands.

"You know that two sparrows are sold for less than a dollar, but not one of those sparrows falls without your Father caring. He knows every hair on your head. So, don't be afraid of those who threaten you. You are of far greater value to your Father than many sparrows."

The warning that Jesus gave his disciples must have been sobering; they and many after them would experience the anger of God's enemies. But there is this consolation: God knows and he cares. That truth has been the comfort of millions who have followed in the steps of these first disciples.

"Everyone who stands with me in the face of opposition, I will stand beside when he comes to stand before my Father who is in heaven. But those who deny me before men I will deny before my Father in heaven."

As I write this in 2016, thousands are standing firm, refusing to deny the Lord in the face of death. On the Internet this morning I read of the martyrdom of Syrian Christians by the ISIS terrorists. Children were beheaded, women raped and killed and their bodies hung on crosses. Men were crucified because they would not give up their hope in Jesus the Messiah. Though ISIS may cut off their heads, they sought the approval of the Lord who has promised to stand beside them when they stand before God. That approval is worth any pain.

34-39. "Don't think that I have come to make peace with the world; no, I have come to stir up things. My coming will stir up a man against his father, and a daughter against her mother, and a daughter-in-law against her mother-in-law.[4] The members of your own family will be your enemies. But the one who loves his father or mother more than he loves me is not worthy to be mine. And whoever loves his son or daughter more than me is not worthy to be mine. If you would come with me, you must pick up your cross and follow me. This is a principle of the Kingdom: The one who values his life more than following me will lose it. But the one who puts his plans and pleasures, even his family, aside for my sake will find real life."

These first disciples must have thought, "Wow! Is this what I am signing up for?"

Why would the disciples be so hated? It was for the same reasons Jesus was hated.

1) Jesus broke all the traditional (man-made) rules, AND he taught people who followed him to do the same. They were to live differently. They were to live genuine rather than fake lives. That was a threat to the religious system.

2) Jesus taught that people should live honest, unselfish, and gentle lives. That was taken as condemnation by those who were choosing to live immoral and dishonest and selfish lives. No one likes to feel condemned.

3) Jesus taught that people have responsibility to God before their responsibility to human rulers or governments. That was a threat to rulers or governments that were not putting God's rules first.

4) Jesus claimed to be God. That meant that people had accountability to him. No one likes to be accountable to someone else. So people reacted in dislike toward Jesus and toward the disciples who were telling them that they were accountable to God.

But, Jesus told them, "God the Father knows what you are going through, and he cares about you." Be encouraged by the fact that what you will be doing is pleasing to God. So even though there will be opposition, even though some people will hate you, be faithful as the messengers of God's Kingdom.

Why would anyone sign up for such a job? The answer is simple. They signed up because they believed that what Jesus was teaching about life was true, that the life he called them to was the real life. Everything else was empty. It was a make-believe game. It was meaningless. They signed up and followed Jesus because they wanted to live in reality. And they signed up to be disciples because they were convinced that what Jesus told them about God was true. God loved them. He wanted them to be his friends. And these disciples were convinced that having God as a friend was worth any price.

> **40-42. "Now, as you go about proclaiming the Kingdom, whoever receives you and your message receives me as well. And the one who welcomes me is welcoming the Father who sent me. Yes, I tell you the one who honors a prophet and the prophet's message will share in the prophet's reward, and the one who honors a man who does what is right will share in his reward. Even if all a man does is give a cup of refreshing cold water to one who is my follower, I assure you, he will not lose his reward."**

What is the reward? It was not status or power in this new Kingdom. Several of the disciples misunderstood and vied among themselves for that place of favour. But Jesus corrected them. It is not that. It is his "well done" that those who faithfully carry the message of the gospel hope for. And that will be more than enough.

FOOTNOTES

1. The word *apostle* means one sent with a message while disciple means a learner.

2. In the Gospel of Mark, Levi (the other name for Matthew) is said to be the son of Alphaeus. Does that mean Matthew and James were brothers? Most Bible experts do not think so. Their fathers simply had the same name.

3. Hospitality to travelers was expected in the Jewish culture. To refuse a traveler would have been a serious insult. `

4. **Micah 7:6**. The quote is not a direct quote from the Septuagint. It is more like a paraphrase. But the reference to Micah is clear. If the context of Micah 7:6 is considered, the implication is that Jesus is alluding to the coming judgment of the nation - represented in Micah 7:4 as the "watchmen." That judgment for their rejection of Messiah Jesus fell upon the Jews in the Jewish-Roman war of 66-73 A.D.

Chapter 11
Building the Kingdom, cont'd

Kinder beim Würfelspiel by Bartolomé Esteban Perez Murillo, c. 1615-1675.
The title translated is *Children Playing Dice*. That seems almost a metaphor for the
way Jesus described the people of his generation.

Matthew in chapter eleven returned to John the Baptist. John was well known to his Jewish readers and was well respected as a prophet. Earlier in chapter three Matthew recorded John's words affirming Jesus as the Messiah the nation hoped for. Now, in chapter eleven Jesus will affirm John as the prophet spoken of in the Hebrew Scriptures, the one who was the forerunner of the Messiah.

Matthew wanted his readers to recognize that the story of Jesus was not a different story from the story of the Hebrew Scriptures; it was a continuation of that story. But Matthew also wanted his readers to understand that Jesus was not simply one more hero in the line of heroes and prophets but was the final one. His story completes the larger story of the Bible. How that can be will become clear as Matthew comes to the end of his Gospel.

We saw earlier in chapter eight that trust and commitment (faith) in the Messiah King is crucial to being a citizen in the Kingdom of Heaven. But not mindless faith, well founded faith. So, in this chapter we see Jesus responding to the doubts of John the Baptist and pointing him to the evidence.

1-6. When Jesus had finished preparing his disciples for their mission, he himself went out to preach and teach in the cities of Galilee.

John, who was in prison,[1] heard about the things Jesus was doing, and he sent some of his disciples to ask Jesus "Are you the one we are expecting, or should we look for someone else?"

John, the one called the Baptist, had baptized Jesus before Jesus began his work of telling people about the Kingdom of God. When John baptized Jesus, John had been confident that Jesus was the Messiah. Now, a year or so later John had been put into prison by the king, and he was having doubts about Jesus.

John sent some of his friends to ask Jesus if he was truly the Messiah. Jesus was gentle in his answer and respectful of John. He did not seem to be troubled by John's doubts.

Jesus replied, "Go back to John and tell him what you have seen and heard. Do not the blind see? Do not the lame walk? Are lepers not cleansed? Do the deaf not hear? Are the dead not raised? Have the poor not had the good news proclaimed to them?" Then Jesus spoke to those gathered around: "Don't let the debate about me confuse you."

Jesus told John's friends to go back to John and tell him what they had seen Jesus doing.

And what had they seen? They had seen Jesus give blind people their sight. They had seen him heal crippled people and even raise dead people to life. And they had heard Jesus preaching to the poor the good news about God's Kingdom.

Those were all things that the prophets had said the Messiah would do. Those things were proof that Jesus was the Messiah. John knew those prophecies. And Jesus knew that the report of what he was doing would satisfy John's doubts.

7-10. After John's disciples left to return to John with this message, Jesus turned to the crowd. "What were you expecting when you went out to John in the wilderness of Judea? Someone who would pat you on the back and tell you how good you are? No? Were you expecting a man dressed in expensive clothes and telling you the secrets of success and prosperity? No? What then? A man who would be straight with you about God's message? Yes. A prophet, and more. This man is the one written about in the Scriptures: *'Look, I am sending my messenger before you, He will prepare the path ahead of you.'"*

Honest doubt is not a bad thing. Do what John did: Check the facts. But there is doubt that is not honest doubt. Jesus will speak about dishonest doubt in verses 16 through 24.

11-15. "I tell you, there has not been a man born greater than John the Baptist. Yet the least important person in the Kingdom of Heaven is greater. [2] From the time when John began to announce the coming of the Kingdom of Heaven to this day, his message has been vigorously debated. Yet those who are serious have pushed past the debate to find in truth the Kingdom John spoke of. The sacred Scriptures, speaking about the Kingdom, spoke of Elijah, who would be the final messenger before the Messiah; and John, if you can accept it, is Elijah. Consider seriously what I say."

Matthew with these words of Jesus directly challenged his Jewish readers to consider carefully who Jesus was. They had heard all the objections, but people who are serious about finding the truth don't allow the criticism or scepticism of others to prevent them from investigating for themselves.

If you search YouTube for any Bible topic, you'll find plenty of sceptical videos. But most of the objections to believing Jesus are warmed-over and oft-repeated criticisms that have been well answered over and over again by knowledgeable believers. But if you look at the comments, most viewers do not bother to investigate for themselves. They repeat the old objections. Push through those. That is what Jesus was saying. Push through. Look for the answers. They are there, and you'll be satisfied that Jesus is the real deal.

16-17. "But what shall I say about the people of this generation? They are like children playing in the streets. They complain saying, 'We played a happy song, and you did not dance. We sang a sad song and you did not cry.'"

Jesus used the words "this generation" when he spoke about dishonest doubt. By that Jesus meant the people who were satisfied with things the way they were and who did not want Jesus or anyone else to shake up their world.

Jesus reminded these people that they had rejected John because he told them they needed to turn away from their sin. They thought John was too harsh. However, when Jesus came telling about the wonderful new freedom of God's Kingdom, they rejected him because they said he was too careless about the religious rules.

The truth was they didn't want anyone changing their lives, not even God. And that is the same reason many people today do not want to hear about Jesus: They don't want Jesus to mess around with their lives.

18-19. "Remember when John came dressed as a prophet, neither eating rich food nor drinking wine; and they said, 'He is possessed by an evil spirit.' Now the Son, of Man has come eating and drinking whatever is set before him, and they say: 'Look! A drunkard and a glutton and a friend of vile cheats and street scum!'[3] But wisdom is proven right by the kind of life it produces."

This kind of doubt is serious. It is scepticism. It is opposition to the truth, and it is the demand that Jesus prove that what he is saying is true - and the refusal to accept the proof that he gives. The result would be eternal judgment for those who chose to reject Jesus and God's message. And the more they understood about Jesus the greater the judgment would be.

20-24. Then Jesus spoke directly to the crowd who had seen his miracles yet had not turned to God. "How great the sadness will be among you people of Chorazin and Bethsaida! If the miracles that have been done in your towns had been done in Tyre and Sidon,[4] they would have long ago turned to God in mourning for their sins. I tell you, it will be better for Tyre and Sidon on the day God judges the earth than for you. And Capernaum, will you escape judgment? No, you too will go down to the place of punishment. For if the great works done in you had been done in Sodom,[5] that city would have repented and avoided the judgment that fell upon it. I tell you, it will be better for the people of Sodom on the day of God's final judgment than for you."

You would think that these people would have taken these words seriously. They believed in God's judgment. They understood how serious it would be. But they loved life the way it was for them, and they were unwilling to turn to God and receive his forgiveness.

25-27. Then thinking of those who had welcomed him and his message of the Kingdom, Jesus was deeply moved and spoke in prayer: "I praise you, Father, Lord of heaven and earth. You have hidden these things from those who think themselves wise and think they have it all figured out and have allowed simple children to understand. Yes. This is your plan." Then to the crowd he said, "The Father has given me full understanding of him. Just as no one really knows me fully except the Father, so no one fully knows the Father except the Son and those to whom the Son chooses to give understanding.

28-29. "But come to me. You who are tired of the senselessness of life, come to me. You who long for more, come to me. Be joined to me. Know me. You will find me a gentle friend, not a tyrant. And you will find the deep rest of mind and heart you long for."

Despite the resistance of these people, Jesus offered them God's mercy once again: "But come to me. . . And you will find the deep rest of mind and heart you long for." He knew that there would be some who would hear him and trust his words and turn from their old life to follow him.

To those people who would give up their old life for the new life, Jesus offered hope. He said they would find "rest for their souls." He meant that they would find what they longed for, forgiveness and a wonderful relationship with God who loved them more than they could ever understand. That friendship with God would be better than anything their old life could give them.

What Jesus said to these people he says to us. If we want a life that is really life, a life that will always satisfy, Jesus will give us that life. It will be a life of peace and friendship with God. It will be excitement and adventure in living a life of purpose beyond any purpose we can make for ourselves. Jesus invites us. The decision is ours.

FOOTNOTES

1. John had been arrested and put in prison by Herod Antipas because John had preached against Herod's marriage to his brother's wife.

2. John saw the Messiah from a distance and in part. But everyone now has the privilege of knowing him fully and personally.

3. The critics found fault with John because he was so severe in his call for repentance. Then when Jesus came preaching God's mercy and love they faulted him for being too easy on sin.

4. Tyre and Sidon were non-Jewish towns along the coast north of Israel.

5. Sodom was the city in the vicinity of the Dead Sea spoken about in Genesis 19 and was notorious for its sin.

Chapter 12

The Kingdom of God Is Present

Jesus Among the Wheatfields by Johannes Raphael Wehle, 1900

Honest doubt leads to searching for the truth. There were many who were not sure what to think of Jesus. They doubted. Jesus always invited them to check him out, to take a closer look. And when they did, they discovered he was the real thing.

There were others, however, whose doubt was really a defense of their own ideas. They were not interested in what was true about Jesus. They were interested in proving that they were right. Chapter twelve is a collection of stories showing where this kind of dishonest doubt takes you.

The first story is about Jesus and his disciples. They were walking through fields of grain on a Sabbath day. They were hungry, so they picked some heads of grain, separated the grain from the husks by rubbing them in their hands, and ate. The Pharisees were angry at this. They said Jesus and his disciples were working on the Sabbath, and that was breaking the Law.

The Pharisees were not really trying to understand why Jesus was doing this. They did not ask; they accused. They were just looking for a reason to find fault in him.

1-2. During those days of ministry in Galilee, Jesus and his disciples traveled from town to town. On one particular day, a Sabbath day, [1] they passed through fields of grain. His disciples were hungry and began to pick a few heads of grain to eat. The religious leaders from the strict sect of the Pharisees saw this and complained: "Look! Your disciples are breaking the Sabbath law."

3-8. Jesus replied, "Haven't you read in the Sacred Scriptures what David did? He and the men with him were hungry, and David went into the house of God where the consecrated bread was laid out before the Lord, and he and his men ate. This was unlawful; only the priests could eat the consecrated bread."

Jesus reminded them that David, whom they held in high esteem as the greatest and most famous king of Israel, had broken the Law at one time when he was hungry. In other words, Jesus took them back to their Scriptures and the Law and showed them that they did not understand God's intentions correctly. The Law was not meant to bind up people in details but to release them to enjoy God's blessings. The Law was about life, not death.

Then he said something that they really did not like. He said that he was greater than the Temple and that he was the Lord of the Sabbath. There could only be one thing greater than the Temple, and there is only one who is Lord of the Sabbath. That is God.

> **"Or haven't you read in the Sacred Scriptures that the priests on duty on the Sabbath in the Temple break the Sabbath laws? Yet they are not guilty. I tell you, something greater than the Temple is here.**

> **"Read Hosea:** *'I desire your love rather than sacrifice. I want you to know me truly rather than to merely bring me offerings.'*[2] **If you only understood what these words mean, you would not judge the innocent. But the Son of Man is Lord, even of the Sabbath."**

There followed another little story like this that served to show that the Pharisees were not honestly trying to figure out who Jesus was. Rather they were trying to find fault in him.

> **9-10. As Jesus came to the town, he joined the Sabbath gathering in the Synagogue. A man was there who had a crippled hand. Looking for opportunity to catch Jesus in some fault, the religious leaders asked, "Is it also lawful to heal on the Sabbath day?"**

> **11-12. Jesus replied, "If any one of you has a sheep that has become trapped in a pit, will he not pull that sheep out, even on the Sabbath? How much more precious is a man than a sheep! Yes, it is lawful to do good on the Sabbath."**

> **13-14. Jesus then said to the man, "Open your hand." So the man opened his hand, and it was fully healed and just as strong as the other. At that the religious leaders began to plot against Jesus and plan how they might kill him.**

Just how far will dishonest doubt take you? This story shows us. It will take you to the place where you will deny the facts before your very eyes.

These men saw the miracle. That was more than enough reason for them, at least, to stop and reconsider their ideas about Jesus. But they did not. Instead, they instantly began to make plans to kill him. It is a reaction that is played out again and again through the story of this gospel. But it is a reaction that is played out in our time, as well.[3]

15-21. Jesus knew what they were plotting and left town, though many people followed him; and he healed them. But he warned them not to speak about him. Jesus' avoidance of controversy fit what Isaiah had spoken about the Messiah:

> *Look, my chosen servant, the one I love and in*
>   *whom I am well pleased.*
> *I will put my Spirit upon him.*
> *He will bring justice to those who are far off.*
> *He won't argue or contend with his opponents.*
> *He will not defend himself.*
> *He will be gentle and will not discourage the*
>   *most faint hearted until justice prevails.*
> *Foreigners will place their faith in him.[4]*

By quoting Isaiah and relating it to Jesus, Matthew reinforced his point to his Jewish readers: Jesus was the Messiah. But the connection between the Old Testament prophecies and Jesus is important for us as well. The fact that Jesus over and over again fulfills prophecy is evidence that he was not some wannabe Messiah. There were plenty of those around, by the way. Showing that Jesus fulfills prophecy demonstrates that he was the one spoken about in the Old Testament. He was the real thing.

22-23. After these things, some brought a man to him who was controlled by an evil spirit and was not able to see or speak, and Jesus healed him so that he could see and speak again. The crowds were amazed and asked, "Could this man be the one God promised, the Son of David?"

There is an irony in this passage. The religious leaders, who should have recognized Jesus as the Messiah and received him joyfully, rejected him and went away and plotted to kill him. The ordinary people, who did not have the knowledge to quickly identify Jesus as the Messiah but who stayed to learn more, were healed.

24. When those from the sect of the Pharisees heard about this healing and the crowds who were speaking of Jesus as possibly the Messiah, they declared, "He commands these evil spirits by the authority of Satan, the chief of demons."

25-37. Jesus knew what they were thinking. And he said to them, "A nation torn by internal discord has no strength to

stand against its enemies, nor can a city or family survive discord. So, if Satan casts out Satan, how will his kingdom be a threat to anyone? But think about it. If I cast out evil spirits by the power of Beelzebub, by whom do your people cast them out? They will be your judges. But if I cast out evil spirits by the Spirit of God, then the Kingdom of God is here."

Jesus warned these men that honest doubt about who he was was okay - just keep thinking and investigating. "Think about it," he told them. But dishonest doubt and opposition to him, when it was clear that what he was doing was being done by the Holy Spirit, amounted to rejection of God himself. That is serious. Rejection of God when you know it is God results in disaster.

"Consider, a thief cannot break into a strong man's house and steal his things unless he ties up the strong man. If the thief does tie up the strong man, then he can easily take whatever he wants from the house.

"Whoever does not rejoice in what I am doing works against me, and whoever does not help me bring people to God is effectively driving people away. It is true that people can be forgiven any sin, even their contemptuous words, but when a person speaks against what the Holy Spirit is obviously doing, he will not be forgiven. Yes, he may even speak ill of the Son of Man, but to defame and reject the Holy Spirit is unforgiveable — It will not be forgiven in this life or in the world that is coming."

The "unforgiveable sin" has been a subject of debate for a long time. What is it? It is the settled rejection of the evidence of the Holy Spirit regarding who Jesus is.

Honest doubt or being uncertain about Jesus is not an unforgiveable sin. Uncertainty often leads to faith. But someone who knows deep down who Jesus is, that he is God's Son and the Savior, and still determines to be his enemy has gone beyond the point of return. That one is beyond repenting. He is beyond the point of forgiveness.

Paul the Apostle was a man who honestly doubted that Jesus was the Messiah. He even worked hard at eliminating the new group of Jesus followers called Christians. But when Jesus appeared to him, that appearance convinced him that he had been wrong. He repented and became one of the most amazing and fearless followers of Jesus in history. He was an honest doubter who only needed the truth. When he had, the truth he changed.

> **"Grow a healthy tree and you'll have good fruit. Grow a diseased tree and you'll harvest unhealthy fruit. You know the health of the tree by looking at the fruit.**
>
> **"You snakes! How can you speak anything that is true when your hearts are so evil? You can speak only what is in your heart. The person whose heart is full of good things will speak the good that is in his heart. The person whose heart is full of evil things will speak the evil that is in his heart. On judgment day you must give account for the things you've spoken, even words spoken without thinking. Those words reveal your heart, and by those words you will be justified or condemned."**

These Pharisees had been nothing but antagonistic to Jesus. Every word had been spoken in condemnation of him. Had their heart been good they would have, at the very least, acknowledged that Jesus had spoken with wisdom (a few did so) and acted with unusual power (a few credited his miracles) and with godly compassion. Even if they were still uncertain in their minds, they would have weighed the evidence. Any reasonable person would do that. But they did not.

That stony refusal to consider Jesus' words and works as God's revealed their heart. It was evil.

> **38-45. Then some of the experts in the Hebrew Scriptures and some from the sect of the Pharisees said to Jesus, "Teacher, we desire to see a miracle to prove you are the Messiah."**

That rebuke caused the Pharisees to be extra angry. They demanded that Jesus do some miracle to prove he is Messiah. They tried to shift the blame for their unbelief to Jesus. But Jesus refused. No miracle would change their minds or hearts. They had already decided. However, Jesus did tell them to expect one more miracle, his death and resurrection. Would they believe then? We know that some did. We also know that others did not.

> **Jesus replied, "Evil and faithless people demand a miracle. But no miracle will be given except the sign of the prophet Jonah. Even as Jonah was entombed three days**

and nights in the belly of the fish, so the Son of Man will be three days and nights entombed in the earth. [They knew very well that Jonah was after three days disgorged by the fish onto dry ground and went on to do what God had given him to do.]

"The people of Nineveh [the city to which the prophet Jonah had been sent with the message of judgment] **will stand in the judgment at your side, and they will be witnesses against you. For they repented when Jonah preached to them, and someone greater than Jonah is speaking to you."**

Would this final miracle, his resurrection, convince them? For some it did, for Luke tells us in Acts that after the resurrection many Pharisees and priests believed. There were evidently many among the religious leaders who had not adamantly made up their minds. And that is a caution to us: We should not cross anyone off the list of those who might be saved, even those who at the moment oppose Jesus. Many of Jesus' greatest enemies have become his faithful followers, Paul the Apostle being among them.

"The queen who came from Sheba[5] will stand as a witness against the people of this time and generation at the judgment. For she came from distant Arabia to hear the wisdom of Solomon, and there is one greater than Solomon here."

Jesus provided one last example of honest doubt - and with it an implied invitation. The queen had heard of God's blessing on King Solomon. But was it real or a fiction? She wanted to know, so her got on her camel and went to find out. What she found convinced her.[6]

Her words, which were well known to the Pharisees and to Matthew's readers are a testimony to honest doubt being rewarded:

She said to the king, "The report I heard in my own country about your achievements and your wisdom is true. But I did not believe what they said until I came and saw with my own eyes."

What was the invitation? Be like the queen and check it out.

Finally, Jesus told them a little story (called a parable) to warn them about what would happen to them. It is a story about a man who had an evil spirit controlling him, but he had gotten rid of it. He had an opportunity now to change his life for the good.

However, the man did not turn away from his evil, so the evil spirit returned with other spirits more evil than he. The result was that the man was in worse shape than before.

"An evil spirit, when it has been expelled from a person, searches for a new home. Finding none, it says, 'I will return to my first home.' Finding the house empty and cleaned, the evil spirit finds seven other spirits more evil than itself, and they move in, and the condition of that person is worse than at the beginning. This is the way it will be for the people of this evil generation."

Jesus was telling the Pharisees that they had a chance to choose God and his Kingdom. But if they did not, they would be opening the door to even worse things in the future. And worse things did happen.

46-50. Now while Jesus was speaking to the crowd, his mother and brothers arrived and were outside wanting to talk to him. Someone told him, "Your mother and brothers are waiting outside wanting to speak to you."

Jesus replied to him, "Who are my mother and brothers? Are not these?" he said, pointing to his disciples. "For whoever is doing the will of my Father in heaven is brother and sister and mother to me."

The chapter ends with a story of Jesus' mother and brothers coming and wanting to see him. We aren't told what they wanted. But it evidently was not as important as what Jesus was engaged in doing at the moment. Jesus' reply to their request was that he was busy. It was not that Jesus did not love his family. But there were many who wanted to see him and hear his message and had not been able to. They had serious questions and serious needs. He could not be distracted by his family's concerns about him.

FOOTNOTES:

1. The Sabbath, which is the last day of the week, was set apart in the Old Testament as holy. No work was allowed. By the Pharisees' strict interpretation of the Law, Jesus and his disciples were breaking the law both by traveling and by picking and eating the grain.

2. Hosea 6. Though Jesus quoted only Hosea 6:6, the Pharisees would have known the context of the verse, which is a scathing rebuke of the religious leaders of Hosea's day. In this case, what Jesus intentionally left unsaid highlighted it and made it the point of his reply.

3. There have many who have approached Jesus with skepticism, yet who have taken the time and done the work of discovery to find out if their first impression was right. Lee Strobel, who was an atheist before doing the research, found Jesus to be the real thing. He has written several books describing the evidence that convinced him. One is *The Case for Christ.* You can find it on Amazon.com.

4. Isaiah 42:1-4

5. The Queen of Sheba, from Ethiopia or Yemen, is mentioned in the ancient literature of the Ethiopians and Arabians.

6. 2 Chronicles 9

Chapter 13

Parables about the Kingdom

The Sower by Vincent van Gogh, 1888

Parables are little stories told to make a point. Jesus is famous for using parables to teach about the upside down kingdom (the Kingdom of God).

Why did Jesus use parables?

1) They were interesting stories. People would listen. The "Parable of the Good Samaritan," for instance, is a widely known and loved story, known even by those who have not read the parable from the Bible.

2) They were puzzles to figure out. People would think about them more than they would think about a lecture or a sermon.

3) They were memorable. People could take one of these little stories with them, remembering it and thinking about it long after Jesus had spoken.

The first parable is called The Parable of the Sower. A sower is a farmer who plants his seeds by scattering them over the plowed ground. The farmer would take a bag of seeds into the field, dip his hand into the seeds, and take that handful of seeds and throw them out ahead of him. However, despite the traditional title, The Parable of the Sower is really more about the ground than about the farmer or the seeds.

1-9. When Jesus had finished teaching he left the house and went to sit by the lake. But a crowd soon gathered around him, so much so that he got into a boat to speak, while the people stood along the shore.

There Jesus spoke many things to them using stories to teach the truths about the Kingdom of Heaven. One of the stories was this one: "A farmer went out into his field to plant seeds. He took the seeds in his hand and scattered them beyond him. As he scattered the seeds, some fell on the hard ground of the path. The birds quickly came and ate these seeds. Some of the seeds fell on ground filled with rocks. They quickly sprouted, but the small plants did not have enough soil in which to put down roots, so they withered in the hot sun. Some fell among weeds. They grew, but so did the weeds, and the weeds choked out the good plants. But other seeds fell on the good ground and grew to maturity and produced a harvest of grain, some a hundred times what had been planted, some sixty times, and some

thirty." Then Jesus said, "Let the one who hears hear carefully."

Jesus did not always explain his parables. But in this case his disciples asked, and he explained the meaning of the story. But first, he explained why he spoke in parables? His explanation is surprising.

10-15. After Jesus finished teaching, the disciples asked, "Why do you speak to people in parables?"

He answered, "You have been chosen to understand the hidden things about the Kingdom of Heaven. But the crowds who have come out of mere curiosity have no real desire to understand, and so the meaning is hidden. There is a principle here: The one who has will be given more, and he will have great understanding. But the one who does not understand and has no desire, even the little he has will be taken from him.

"This is why I speak to the crowds in parables. *'They are hard of heart and have no ability to understand these spiritual truths.'*

"In fact, here the words of God to Isaiah the prophet have come to pass:
'They will hear but not understand what they hear,

They will see, yes, but not understand what they see.'

For their heart has become dull, and their eyes are closed,

So that they may neither see nor hear and understand

And turn from their sins, that I would heal them.'"[1]

What a strange answer! It sounds like Jesus is deliberately hiding the message of the Kingdom of Heaven from the crowd. Wasn't it for the purpose of revealing the coming of the Kingdom that he taught them?

The answer is, yes; he wanted them to know and understand. But people can reach such a point in their rejection of God's message that God takes radical action. That was the case in Isaiah's day when God gave Isaiah these instructions.

God instructed Isaiah to speak to the people these very words that Jesus used.

For what purpose? To incite them to listen. They were a people doomed to destruction because of their disobedience and their unwillingness to listen to God. As a last resort, God declares through Isaiah that they will not hear or understand or turn to God in repentance. Perhaps that message would be such a shock to them that they would hear.

Likewise, Jesus was not counting his hearers as hopeless. But they were close. This parable he spoke, if they would only hear, was pretty extreme and in their face. It was a last resort to provoke their attention.

But not everyone was unwilling; many were searching for the truth. Some wanted to understand, and they would respond in faith. To these - and his disciples were among them - Jesus spoke plainly.

16-17. But to his disciples Jesus said, "Your eyes are blessed, for you do see and understand, and your ears are blessed, for they hear. Here's the truth: Many prophets and upright people in the past longed to see what you see and did not have that privilege and to hear what you hear and did not hear it."

Because the disciples honestly desired to hear the truth about the Kingdom from Jesus and because they would respond to it in faith, he explained to them this parable.

18-23. "Listen, then, to the meaning of this story about the farmer: When anyone hears the message of the Kingdom and does not value what he hears, the evil one comes like the birds and takes away any understanding of the message. This is the meaning of the seeds that fell upon the path.

"The seeds that fell on rocky, shallow ground and do not survive show what happens when those who eagerly receive the message of God's Kingdom are turned away from obeying it when they run into the mockery of scoffers or persecution from those who oppose the message.

"The seeds that fell among the weeds picture those who hear the message and begin on the path of obedience but finally are turned aside to live for the things that absorb the interest of the people around them. They are stunted by their desire for the rich life. Though they hear, the message, it results in nothing.

"But the seeds that fell on good, receptive ground illustrate the person who hears the message of the Kingdom and welcomes it. The result is a life of faith that produces a great crop, sometimes as much as a hundred times what the farmer planted, sometimes sixty, and sometimes thirty."

Some people don't listen at all. Some people think the message is good, but they are afraid to obey it because of the scorn of their friends. Some people think the message is good, but they let other things become more important. But some people hear the message and are convinced it is true and important. They do what Jesus says. They are the good soil.

Jesus told this story not to judge those who do not follow him or who turn back after beginning. He told the story to make this point: Be good soil by listening and doing what I tell you.

The second parable is called The Parable of the Weeds. It answered the question people had about how God will separate people who really belong to the Kingdom of God from those who don't. The problem was that they can look a lot alike.

24-30. Jesus, speaking further about the Kingdom of God, said, "The Kingdom of Heaven is like this: A farmer had his hired men plant his field with good seeds. But during the night while his men were asleep, an enemy came secretly and planted weeds in his wheat field. So, when the plants began to sprout and grow up to bear heads of grain, so did the weeds. The hired men came to the owner of the field and said to him, 'Sir, didn't you give us good seeds to plant in your field? How is it that now the field is full of weeds?'

"The farmer replied, 'This is the work of my enemy.' The hired men asked, 'Do you want us to go into the fields and pull the weeds?' But the famer told them no. 'If you do,

you'll pull up some of the wheat along with the weeds. Let both the weeds and the wheat grow until the harvest. Then I will tell the harvesters to gather the weeds first and tie them into bundles to be burned. But I'll have them store the wheat in my barn.'"

Jesus would explain the meaning of this parable later. Before he did, he told two more parables, The Parable of the Mustard Seed and The Parable of the Yeast. These answer the question about the success of the Kingdom of Heaven.

31-35. Jesus told them another parable: "The Kingdom of Heaven is like a mustard seed, which a farmer planted in his field. A mustard seed is the smallest of all seeds, yet it grows into the largest plant in the field. It becomes like a tree; birds come and perch on its branches."

Then he told them another parable: "The Kingdom of Heaven is like the yeast a woman mixed into a large quantity of flour, working the dough until it was thoroughly kneaded."

Jesus spoke these truths to the crowd in stories. In fact, he spoke to them only in parables. In doing so, what the prophet foretold was done: *I will speak in a parable; I will speak things hidden since the creation of the world.*"[2]

Most Jews figured the Kingdom of Heaven would include pretty much every Jew. They were, after all, sons of Abraham. Yet here was Jesus, the Messiah King - or so he implied. But not many Jews were really following him except out of curiosity. This Messiah and his Kingdom didn't look like it was going anywhere. Was he really the Messiah King? Was this really God's Kingdom he was promoting? If so, why was it so poorly received? But Jesus assured them the Kingdom of Heaven would grow to be very large, larger than they imagined, and would ultimately spread through all the people groups of the world.

The people to whom Matthew wrote in the mid-first century had begun to see the Kingdom of Heaven grow as many, both non-Jews and Jews from around the Mediterranean world, became followers of Jesus. But that was only a beginning. There was a world beyond. Matthew, in fact, wrote this story of Jesus for his Jewish congregations because he was getting ready to go east to a part of the world that had not yet heard of Jesus or the Kingdom of Heaven. The point of the parables was that many would receive the message - and they would not all be Jews.

Matthew in his selection of parables implied that the followers of Jesus have a mission. It is to take the message into the entire world. The Parable of The Yeast underscores that mission: As we take the message of Jesus and the Kingdom of God into the entire world, it will be received and obeyed, and it will grow to be very large.

36. When he finished teaching, Jesus left the crowds and went into the house where his disciples asked him privately: "Tell us the meaning of the story of the weeds in the field of wheat."

The disciples were not sure what Jesus meant in the parable,. and they were concerned because there was a danger to be avoided, and they wanted to be sure where they stood.

37-39. Jesus explained, "The farmer who planted the good seeds is the Son of Man. The field is the world. The good seeds are the people who belong to the Kingdom of Heaven. The weeds are the people who belong to the evil one. And the enemy who planted them is the devil. The harvest stands for the judgment at the end of the age, and the harvesters are angels.

40-43. "At the end of the age the weeds will be pulled up and burned in the fire. The Son of Man will send his angels to weed out of the Kingdom all who cause sin and do evil. The angels will throw them into the blazing furnace where there will be cries of sorrow and grinding of teeth. But the righteous will shine like the sun and find their home in the Kingdom of their Father. Listen carefully to what I say."

The disciples did well to ask, for this parable explains what must have been a puzzle to them and has been a puzzle to many Christians since. It explains why God does not immediately have the false followers of Jesus removed. The answer is that any attempt by us (the hired men) to purify the church by removing everyone who is not a genuine Christian would catch up many genuine Christians in the purge. We could not possibly know who was genuine and who was not.

But the angels whom God will have do the separating of the good and the evil will know.

There is a final important truth in this parable: The final judgment will seal the future of all. The righteous will forever enjoy their home in the Kingdom of God. The evil will be forever consigned to sorrow.

The next two parables, called The Hidden Treasure and The Pearl, are about how valuable the Kingdom of Heaven is. Belonging to the Kingdom would be worth any price you would have to pay.

44. He told them another parable: "The Kingdom of Heaven is like a great treasure that has been hidden in a field. When a man finds it, he leaves it and goes and sells all his possessions so that he can buy the field and own the treasure.

45-46. "Again, the Kingdom of Heaven is like a very expensive pearl. A merchant who seeks such treasures, when he finds the pearl, sells everything he owns to buy it."

The last parable is called The Net. It is Jesus' final warning. At the end of this age, the age in which people have a chance to choose to belong to God's Kingdom or the kingdom of this world, God will separate people into two groups. One group will enjoy God's Kingdom forever. The other will suffer terrible loss forever.

47-50. "And again, the Kingdom of Heaven is like a net which fishermen cast into the sea. It gathers fish of every kind; and when it is pulled ashore, the fishermen collect the good fish and throw away the bad."

This parable is like the parable of the weeds in the field of wheat. Why would Matthew include both parables? No doubt because the warning implied in them was very serious. To Matthew's Jewish readers it was a warning that they should not rely on their being Jews and thereby being God's people. It was essential that they be sure they are truly God's people rather than God's people in name only.

To Christians today it is essential that we not rely on our Christian connections. Growing up in a Christian home does not make anyone a genuine Christian. Nor does belonging to a church or living in a Christian culture. What marks Christians as genuine is that they are righteous. And such *righteousness* is the result of being forgiven because they have personally trusted in Jesus as their Savior. The effect is that their lives begin to reflect their faith as they do that which is right.

"This is the way it will be at the end of the age. The angels will separate the evil from the righteous, and they will throw the evil into the fire where there will be cries of sorrow and grinding of teeth."

51-52. Then Jesus asked his disciples, "Do you understand these things?" They answered, "Yes." To which Jesus replied, "Every student of Scripture who has learned the secrets of the Kingdom of Heaven is like a homeowner who decorates his house with valuable things both old and new."

Many of the things Jesus taught were not new. They were found in the Hebrew Scriptures and had been part of the faith of Israel for centuries. But there were things that were new. Jesus was new. The things he taught about following him were new. The things he taught about trust in him for salvation were new. The disciples would need to bring the old and the new together, as would Matthew's Jewish readers.

53-58. When Jesus had finished teaching his disciples these things, he left the house where they had been staying and continued his travels ending at Nazareth, his hometown. There he taught in the weekly religious gathering at the synagogue.

The chapter ends with a sad story. Jesus returned to his home town, the town where he lived as a child and as a young man. The people in his town remembered him. And they could not believe this man whom they knew so well could be the Messiah or could do miracles. Because they did not believe in him, Jesus did not do many miracles there.

His teaching astonished those who had known him, and they asked among themselves: "Where has this man gained this strange wisdom? How does he do these miracles we hear about? Isn't this the carpenter's son? Isn't his mother Mary, and aren't his brothers James and Joseph and Simon and Jude? And his sisters, are they not living here among us? Where did he come by all these new things he teaches?" They thought him presumptuous, and they rejected him.

Jesus said to them, "A prophet is honored everywhere except in his hometown and by his own family." Because

they rejected him, he did not do many miraculous things among them.

We are again impressed with the importance of belief. But the story begs the question why. Why was Jesus limited by the belief of people? Or was he? The passage does not say he could not do miracles. It says he did not do miracles. The difference is that miracles without faith become merely a carnival sideshow. People who are inclined toward skepticism attribute them to trickery not to God's power. And Jesus was not interested in putting on a show.

Each of these parables emphasized how important it is to take Jesus' message seriously. God made us for this purpose, that we might enjoy him and his blessings forever. But we can refuse LIFE. If we refuse LIFE by choosing to live only for the things in this life, The result will be terrible when this life is over.

Jesus told these parables to urge people to choose life.

FOOTNOTES
1. Isaiah 6:9, 10, quoted directly from the Greek Septuagint translation of the Hebrew Scriptures.

2. Psalm 78:2. The word in Hebrew translated *parable* here is *machal*. It means a word of wisdom or a proverb. Jesus intentionally uses parables, Matthew noted, to call attention to the fact that he is speaking wisdom about the Kingdom of Heaven.

Chapter 14
Son of God

Historical picture of Tiberias from the early 1900s.
It was the capital city of King Herod in the time of Jesus.

Matthew was painting the portrait of the Messiah one brush stroke at a time. Jesus is first introduced to his Jewish readers as a king in the family line of David, then as a miracle baby, then as the fulfillment of the Old Testament prophecies of the Messiah, then as having the power and authority of God. But there is one more thing. It is the thing that Jews instinctively drew back from because of their absolute monotheism (belief that there is only one God). It was that Jesus is God.

The idea that God would have a Son who was as much God as God the Father was unbelievable for Jews. It was pagan. And for someone to claim to be equal to the Father or to allow that claim to be made was a high crime. So, Matthew brought his Jewish readers to that truth gradually and through the eyes of the disciples rather than stating it outright.

The thing that brought the disciples to that realization is the subject of this chapter.

1-2. It was at that time that Herod Antipas, the Tetrarch[1] ruling the region of Galilee, began to hear reports about Jesus and the miracles he was doing. Herod said to his attendants, "This must be John the Baptist. He has come back from the dead. That is why he is able to do these miraculous things."

3-12. Herod's acquaintance with John was this: When John had accused Herod of violating the Jewish law by marrying Herodias, the wife of Herod's brother Philip, Herod had ordered John arrested and imprisoned. Herod had planned to put John to death, but he was afraid that the people of Galilee, who regarded John as a prophet, would rise up in rebellion.

However, at Herod's birthday celebration, Herodias's daughter danced for Herod and the guests, and this so pleased Herod that he promised with an oath to give her whatever she wanted as a reward. At her mother's urging she asked, "Give me the head of John the Baptist on a platter."

Herod was disturbed. But because he had sworn an oath before the dinner guests, he granted her request and had John beheaded in his prison cell. John's head was brought to the girl, and she gave it to her mother.

John's disciples came and buried the body and then went to tell Jesus.

13-14. When Jesus heard about John's death, he left the place where he had been teaching and crossed the lake by boat to find a place away from the crowds where he could be by himself.

Jesus knew that John's work was finished. God's purpose for John was that he announce the coming of the Messiah. Now the Messiah had come. John had done what God had given him to do. Even John had said that now the attention of people must be upon the Messiah and not upon him (John 3:30).

Still, Jesus was saddened at the news of John's death. John was a cousin of Jesus. But more than that, John was a man whom Jesus highly regarded and loved as friend, as a prophet, and as a faithful servant of God. Jesus grieved.

It was for that reason he wanted to get away from the crowds and have some private time.

But the people learned where he was going and followed him on foot from all the cities around the lake. When Jesus saw the crowd that had followed him and especially those who came with illnesses hoping for healing, he put aside his own grief for John and out of compassion healed them.

15-21. When it was getting late in the day, the disciples came to Jesus and said to him, "This is a remote place, and the day is getting late. Should you not send the crowd away so they can find food for themselves in the villages?"

But Jesus said to them, "They don't need to leave. Give them something to eat yourselves."

The disciples replied, "We only have five loaves of bread and two fish."

"Bring those loaves and fish to me," he said. Then Jesus had the crowd sit down on the grass, and he took the five loaves of bread and two fish and, looking up to heaven, blessed God [2] and then he broke the loaves and gave the pieces to the disciples. The disciples gave the pieces out to

the crowd, and they ate until they were full. When everyone was finished, the disciples gathered up the pieces that remained – twelve baskets full. Now, the number of those who had eaten was about five thousand, not counting the women and children.

Matthew did not say how all that happened or tell us what the disciples thought.

Miracles do not always happen instantly, like magic. Sometimes they seem quite natural, just as the bread in the baskets. Perhaps taking one loaf out simply did not subtract from the number in the basket. It was not that the basket suddenly filled up; it may have been that the loaves never ran out. In any event, the disciples remembered this unusual event. However, it did not change their lives as dramatically as the next experience did.

22-33. As soon as the leftover bread had been gathered, Jesus had his disciples get back into the boat and go ahead of him to the other side of the lake. He himself sent the crowds home. As night came, he went up into the hills to be alone and to pray.

In the middle of the night, the boat with the disciples was out on the lake several miles from shore. A wind had kicked up the waves and was making it difficult for the disciples to make any progress. Around four in the morning, Jesus came walking toward them on the lake.

The disciples were terrified when they saw him. "It is a ghost!" they screamed in fear. But Jesus spoke to them. "Don't be afraid. It is I."

Then Peter called out to him, "Lord, if it is you, command that I may come to you on the water."

At that, Jesus said, "Come." So Peter got out of the boat and walked toward Jesus. But when he saw the waves around him and the wind, he grew fearful. As he began to sink, he called out in fear, "Lord, Save me!"

Jesus immediately stretched out his hand and took hold of him. "You have too little faith, he said. "Why did you not trust in me?"

We have turned this story into a parable of trusting Jesus whenever things get rough. That is okay. But in that moment this experience grabbed these men roughly by the shoulders, stood them on their feet, and slapped them around. It was that real.

Up to this point, they had been spectators. What they had seen and heard had been impressive, for sure. But with this, they were at the epicenter of an earthquake that shattered their comfortable Jewish worldview. This man Jesus was not only Messiah, King, and Prophet. He was God.

Too little faith? No kidding.

Christians have tried to describe the unimaginable truth that Jesus is both man and God for centuries. The Nicene Creed of the fourth century has perhaps been the best. But it still fails to capture what the disciples suddenly realized. This was big. This was personal.

When Jesus and Peter stepped into the boat, the winds died down. Astounded at this miracle, the disciples bowed before him and worshiped him saying "Without a doubt, you are the Son of God."

The whole experience of Jesus walking on the water - and Peter also - was enough to convince these men that Jesus was truly extraordinary. Who could do these things but God, or the Son of God?

Their response was to worship him.

What they had seen and experienced drove them to that conclusion. Even then it was not a conclusion they could fully put their heads around, as we see later.

34-36. In the calm they completed their journey across the lake to the region of Galilee. When they disembarked, the people living in that place recognized Jesus, and they sent word to the surrounding area. Again the people brought to him all their sick and infirm and asked to simply touch the border of his robe. And as many as did were healed.

FOOTNOTES

1. A Tetrarch is a governor of a region divided into four governorships. Herod Antipas ruled as Tetrarch the region of Galilee west of the lake of Galilee, which included Nazareth, and the area east of the Jordan River, the place where John the Baptist had carried on his work. Herod's capital city during the time of Jesus was Tiberias, situated on the west shore of the Lake of Galilee. The location where Jesus went to find some quiet in verse 13 was outside the region ruled by Herod.

2. Jesus probably prayed something similar to the traditional Jewish blessing: "Blessed are you, Lord our God, who brings forth bread from the earth."

Chapter 15
The Law of the Kingdom

Jesus and the Canaanite Woman by Mattia Preti, c. 1660.

It is becoming clear by this point in Matthew's Gospel that Jesus was a divide. Like the continental divide in the Rocky Mountains where the water that falls on the mountains goes either to the west or to the east, Jesus was the point of divide among people. They either resisted and rejected him and went off toward destruction or they turned to him and received him and began their journey toward God.

In this chapter, those two kinds of people are described.

1-2. While still in Galilee teaching and healing, Jesus was visited by some experts in the Law and some from the religious sect of the Pharisees from Jerusalem. They asked him, "Why do your disciples ignore the traditions passed down to us by our elders and not wash their hands[1] before eating?"

The first group to confront Jesus was the Pharisees and teachers from Jerusalem. They came to Jesus to complain that he and his disciples were not following the religious rules that "good" Jews followed: The disciples did not wash their hands before eating. Religious Jews washed their hands not because they might be dirty but because they might have touched something that was religiously unclean or bad. That uncleanness needed to be washed off before they ate.

Jesus pointed out to them that these were the rules that men had made. The rules that God made for living were far more important. And the Pharisees were breaking those rules.

3-9. But Jesus responded, "Why do you break God's Law by your traditions? You fail to honor your father or mother. Though God commanded that you should honor your father and mother and that whoever curses his father or mother is guilty of a crime worthy of death, you say that whoever declares to his father or mother this money is a gift I give to God, so I can't help you (and thereby fails to care for his father or mother), is free of that obligation."

One of the rules God had given was to take care of your mother and father in their old age. But the Pharisees had found a way to avoid that. It cost too much to take care of your family. So they made a rule that any money that was dedicated to God could not be used to care for the family. It was God's. But the thing was, that money could be used by the Pharisee until he got around to giving it to God. So the only thing this man-made rule did was make it possible to disobey God.

It was hypocrisy. The Pharisees looked very religious, but they were not following God's rules at all.

"You frauds! Isaiah had it right when he wrote, '*These people confess their faith in me with their mouth, but their hearts are not in tune with me at all. Their worship is all about following their own man-made rules.*'"[2]

Jesus wanted to clarify for the crowd what he had just said about unclean foods: Religious ceremonies do not even come close in importance to the condition of the heart and the words we speak that reveal the heart.

10-11. Having finished admonishing these fakes, Jesus called the crowd to him and said, "Listen carefully. The food that goes into your mouth does not make you unclean. But what comes out of your mouth can."

Jesus' words, however, offended these "important men."

12-20. Then his disciples came to Jesus and spoke about their concern. "Don't you know that these men from the sect of the Pharisees were offended by what you said?"

Jesus replied, "The plants that my heavenly Father have not planted will be pulled up roots and all. These men have chosen their path; let them walk in it. They are blind guides, and blind men follow them. If a blind man leads a blind man, they both fall into the ditch."

These words seem harsh. Is Jesus crossing these men off as unredeemable and beyond hope? The answer is that he is speaking not about any individual but about anyone who has crossed the divide and has set his mind and heart to oppose God. These are unredeemable. But there were many individuals among the Pharisees who were genuinely seeking God. They would eventually find him, as Nicodemus and Paul the apostle did, both of whom became followers of Jesus..

Then Peter [evidently perplexed] **asked Jesus to explain the parable. Jesus replied to Peter, "Are you still without spiritual perception? Don't you know that whatever you eat goes into the mouth and into the belly and out into the toilet? But the words that come out of your mouth come**

from the inner man, the heart; those words and the thoughts behind them are what make a man unclean. For it is out of the heart that such evil things as murders, adulteries, sexual immoralities, thefts, lies, and words of contempt come. These are what make a man unclean. But don't fall for this silliness that eating with hands that have not been ceremonially washed make you unclean."

The second group of people in this chapter was represented by a Canaanite woman. She was not a Jew, and the Jews thought her a worthless sinner. But this woman showed more real faith than the Pharisees.

The point of this contrast between the Pharisees and the Canaanite woman was to show that God is more interested in real faith and trust than in mere religious activity. But it also showed that God is interested in any person, Jew or not, who has faith in him.

21-28. After this confrontation with the Pharisees, Jesus left Galilee for the coast and the region of Tyre and Sidon. While he and his disciples were there a woman of Canaan found them and, knowing of Jesus, she repeatedly cried to him, "Have mercy, O Lord, Son of David. My daughter is troubled by an evil spirit."[3] But Jesus did not answer her. Finally his disciples, who were tired of her constant cries, asked Jesus to send her away.

Jesus answered them, "I am sent to the lost sheep of the family of Israel."

But the woman, hearing this, refused to be put off. She came and worshiped him and said again, "Lord, help me."

Jesus answered, "It is not right to take the bread prepared for the children and give it to the dogs."

But she replied, "Yes, Lord. But do not the dogs eat the crumbs that fall from the master's table?"

The way this conversation went suggests that Jesus was not addressing the woman. He was speaking to his disciples. And he was reflecting what they were thinking, that God is only interested in Jews. Being in what they considered enemy territory, they must have been unusually aware of these non-Jewish "pagans." We can almost see them nodding in agreement with what Jesus said.

But the woman's repeated request tugs at the heart, perhaps even the hearts of the disciples. Still, Jesus repeats a refusal. Maybe a little more tentatively this time. Maybe he is reflecting the change in the disciples' hearts.

The woman replied to what she overheard, and her reply was riveting: "We may be no better than dogs, but can we not have the scraps?"

Up to this point Jesus was doing a little serious tongue-in-cheek probing of his disciples' hearts. But here Jesus addressed her.

Jesus was amazed at her answer. "Dear woman," he said, "you have great faith. What you ask will be yours." And from that moment her daughter was healed.

The Scripture says Jesus was amazed at her faith. But he was also pleased with her persistence. The kind of faith that pleased him was a faith that trusted who he was and what he could do and would not let go until it was satisfied.

29-31. After this Jesus left the coast and returned to the region of Galilee. He went up into a mountain along the lake. A large crowd gathered, and he sat and taught them. The people brought to him those who were lame and blind and mute and injured, as well as others who were infirm. They placed them at Jesus' feet, and he healed them all. The people marveled when they saw the mute speak and the injured made whole and the lame walk and the blind see. And they praised the God of Israel for such wonders.

These people, like the Canaanite woman, were coming to Jesus because they had a need, and they believed he could help. They were sick or blind or they were simply hungry to know God. And Jesus healed them and fed them and told them who God truly is.

The result of their faith was that they went away satisfied. Jesus met their need.

32-38. Then once again as Jesus saw the multitude who had been with him for three days without eating, he had compassion for them. He called his disciples to him and said, "I am concerned for these people; they have been here

with me for three days and have had nothing to eat. I will not tell them to leave; they may suffer from hunger and collapse along the way."

But his disciples replied, "Where can we find enough bread in this remote place to feed this many people?"

To that Jesus replied, "How much food do you have with you?"

They answered, "We have only seven loaves of bread and a few small fish."

Jesus took the bread and the fish and said to the crowd, "Sit down." And he gave thanks and broke the loaves into pieces and gave the pieces to his disciples who distributed them among the people. Everyone ate his fill, and the disciples gathered up the leftovers, seven baskets full. The number of those who were fed was four thousand men, not counting the women and children. After the crowd had eaten and the pieces were gathered, Jesus sent the people home. He himself got into a boat in order to sail to the region of Magdala on the west side of the lake.

Some critics have suggested that Matthew got a little mixed up and told the same story about feeding the crowd twice. Or maybe he picked up two variations of the same story and included both in his Gospel. But that assumes Matthew was not there as a participant - though we have every reason to believe he was.

It assumes also that the two stories of the feeding of the crowds were placed in the narrative as random stories in a collection of random, loosely connected stories. But that idea ignores the obvious care Matthew used in weaving the narrative of this Gospel together. There is nothing that is random.

And it ignores the context. Each of these miracles is recounted because it fits the purpose of the narrative. Here this story is in counterpoint to the lack of faith among the Pharisees: The crowds, at least, were attracted to Jesus. And their faith, even if it was tentative, was satisfied.

What about the extra bread? Both stories of Jesus feeding the crowds say that there was bread left over. Various interpretations have been offered. Perhaps it is best to simply notice that when God blesses, his blessing is abundant.

FOOTNOTES

1. This rule, hand washing, was not part of the instructions given in the Old Testament. And it had nothing to do with physical cleanliness. It was ceremonial and traditional. It represented ritual purification. It was part of the Temple worship. It had never been made a practice of ordinary life. But here it is taken to the extreme, as the zealous religious leaders often did, and made a law apparently equal in force to God's laws.

2. Isaiah 29:13. Isaiah wrote these things to the people of his generation who had turned away from God and were headed toward God's judgment and abandonment two generations later. The warning Jesus spoke to them by referring to this passage is that they too are headed toward God's judgment and abandonment, a judgment that fell upon the Jews in 70 A.D. As is often the case, the context of the verse quoted adds to the impact of the quote. Verse fourteen says that God will "astound them with wonder after wonder and thereby destroy the wisdom of those who think themselves wise and intelligent." That is exactly what Jesus did.

3. The Greek text describes this spirit as a devil.

Chapter 16
The King in His Glory

The Handing-over the Keys A tapestry by Raphael, 1515 – 1516, Victoria and Albert Museum, London.

The religious leaders of the Jews were now firm in their opposition to him. On one level they saw him as undermining their position and authority with the people. On another level they hated him because he has exposed their hypocrisy.

They make one last demand.

1-4. Some of the religious leaders from the Pharisees along with some Sadducees from the Temple priests followed Jesus seeking to force him into some misstep. As he was getting ready to depart in the boat, they demanded of him some miraculous sign from heaven to prove that he was the Messiah.

Jesus answered their insulting demand by saying, "When there is a red sunset, you predict that the next day will be clear. When the sky is red and cloudy at the sunrise, you predict the day will be stormy. You do well. But you are not able to see or understand the signs that warn you of the crisis ahead for this generation. This is indeed an evil and faithless generation of people. They ask for a sign; but no sign will be given them, except the sign of the prophet Jonah." At that he left them and departed in the boat.

The Pharisees demanded a miracle that would prove that Jesus was the Messiah. But Jesus refused to show them a miracle. Instead he told them that they should have been able to understand from what they had already seen and heard. He had shown them many miracles that only the Messiah could do. Now He told them that he will provide only one more miracle for them. He called it the "sign of Jonah."

That must have been a puzzle. What could that mean?

In fact, no one knew until it happened. Then the disciples understood what the final and most important miracle was, and so did the religious leaders. It was his resurrection. That would be the sign.

5-12. When Jesus and his disciples arrived at Magdala on the shore of Galilee, they realized they had forgotten to bring any bread. At just that moment Jesus spoke and said to them, "Beware of the yeast of the Pharisees and the Sadducees." The disciples connected this to the fact that they had forgotten to bring bread and thought Jesus was

scolding them. But Jesus knowing what they were thinking, said to them, "Do you have such little faith? Are you worried about failing to bring bread? Think. Don't you remember the five loaves that fed five thousand people? How much was leftover? Or do you not remember the seven loaves that fed four thousand people? And how many basketsful of leftover pieces did you pick up?

"Don't you understand that I was not speaking of bread but about the yeast of the Pharisees and Sadducees?" Then they understood that Jesus was not talking about actual bread or yeast but about the influence of the Pharisees and Sadducees.

By now the religious leaders were so firmly against Jesus that they would not change their minds. So Jesus warned his disciples that they not be misled by the religious leaders' arguments and teachings against him. He called that the "yeast of the Pharisees."

13-20. Sometime later after Jesus and his disciples had traveled to Caesarea Philippi[1] he asked them about what they had been hearing: "Whom do the people say that the Son of Man is?"

It has now been three years since Jesus had begun to speak to people and to call people into the Kingdom of Heaven. His twelve disciples have been with him most of that time. Jesus wanted to know what they thought of him.

He asked them first what other people were saying. Then he asked what they thought.

The disciples answered: "Some are saying you are John the Baptist. Others think you are Elijah or Jeremiah or one of the other prophets."

Jesus then asked them, "And who do you say I am?"

Simon Peter replied, "You are the Messiah, the Son of the living God."

The Son of the living God! That was as bold an answer as any Peter could have given.

If anyone knew Jesus, it was Peter. He had come to this conclusion that Jesus was the Son of the living God because of what he had seen Jesus do and what he had heard him say. But Jesus told him that was not the only reason. The most important reason was that God had told him - in his heart.

"You are greatly privileged, Simon son of Jonah," Jesus said to Peter. "You have not come to this understanding by human reasoning; rather it is my Father in heaven who has revealed this to you."

What does that mean?

It means that even if we have all the evidence necessary for coming to the conclusion that Jesus is the Son of God, we need something more. We need the inner conviction or belief that it is true. Only God gives that.

Without that strong belief, Jesus is just an interesting fact. He is a fact like the fact that Mao Zedong led a revolution in China or that George Washington was the first President of the United States. We can debate or talk about facts. But if Jesus is the Son of God, we cannot merely talk about him. He cannot merely be the subject of debate. The only reasonable thing is to kneel before him and worship him. The only thing that makes sense is to follow him.

We only come to the point of believing in Jesus that way when God reveals who he really is in our hearts, the place of our deepest and truest thoughts and emotions.

"I name you Peter, a stone," Jesus continued, "and so you are. And upon this rock I will build my congregation of the faithful."

Christians have debated the meaning of these words for centuries. Catholic Christians believe Jesus was saying that Peter would be the foundation of the church. Protestant Christians believe that Jesus was saying the *declaration* that "Jesus is the Son of the living God" was the foundation of the church.

Certainly the latter of the two has been true for both Catholics and Protestants: The foundational truth and the message of the church has always been that "Jesus is the Son of God."

"And the 'Gates of Hades' shall not win in the conflict of the ages."

It happened that Jesus and the disciples were standing at the Gates of Hell as they were having this conversation. The Gates of Hell was a spring that flowed out of the rock at the base of Mt. Hermon. Worshipers of the Greek god Pan had built a shrine there because they believed the spring was the door to the underworld.

Jesus' point was that the underworld and all the power of Satan would not be able to successfully oppose the message that "Jesus is the Son of God" and would not be able to stand before the church as it proclaimed freedom from all that holds people back from knowing God and his power - in the Messiah.

"I will give you the keys of the Kingdom of heaven, and whatever evil power you all bind on earth will be bound by my heavenly Father, and whatever cords of bondage you all loose on earth will be loosed by my heavenly Father." Then he strictly told his disciples not to tell anyone that he was the Messiah.

This was a strong promise. It was spoken directly to Peter, who had just responded to Jesus' question about who he was. Catholic Christians see that as a declaration that Peter would have an unusual role in the church as the first Pope and that this authority would pass on to the men who followed Peter as Popes.

History may leave us with a different interpretation, however. Authority over the powers of darkness and authority to bind Satan and to loose those who have been bound by Satan has been given the men and women throughout history who boldly claim this promise as theirs. It has not been the province of the Pope alone.

21-23. From that time on Jesus began to explain to his disciples how he must go to Jerusalem and suffer the wrath of the religious leaders from among the elders and the priests and the Scribes, who were the so called experts in the Hebrew Scriptures. He explained that he would be killed but would be raised to life again on the third day after his death.

If you think about it, the idea of the Son of God dying was crazy. If Jesus was the Messiah who would save the nation and bring in a time of peace, how could that happen if Jesus died?

It was crazy in another way. How could the Son of God die? That seemed impossible.

Peter was aghast and took Jesus aside to lecture him. "Lord," he said, "don't talk that way. This will never happen." But Jesus turned to Peter and spoke to him face to face. "Get behind me, Satan!" he said. "You are putting your own desires ahead of God's plans, and you are making it difficult for me."

24-28. Then Jesus spoke to all of the disciples: "If you are going to follow me, you will need to put your own ideas and advantages and even your life aside and pick up your cross and follow me to death."

At that point Jesus told his disciples something that was so contrary to the way we usually think that it took the disciples a long time to understand it. That was that they too must die if they were to be true disciples.

Jesus meant they must make everything that was important in this life of no importance compared to living for God and others.

He told them the reward for doing that would be great. But it was still a hard saying to accept.

"The truth is," Jesus continued, "that trying to save your life will result in losing it, but losing your life to follow me will result in your finding real life. What is the advantage, even if you have everything you desire in this world, if you lose your eternal soul? When it comes right down to it, what could possibly come close to the value of your eternal soul? For the Son of Man is going to come, clothed in the glory of his Father. He will reward each person based on what he has done. Indeed," Jesus told them, "some of you will not come to the end of life before they see the Son of Man coming clothed in the glory of his Kingdom."

FOOTNOTES
1. This was a place no good Jew would visit. It was the location of the shrine of the god Pan. Jesus' taking his disciples there was like bearding the lion in his den. It was taking the fight to the very fortress of the enemy.

Chapter 17

The King's Glory Revealed

Transfiguration of Jesus, Poland, Mielno, church, stained glass

Remember that Matthew has been leading his readers to see that Jesus was the Messiah the Jews expected. But he also wanted to expand their idea of who the Messiah was, for Jesus was far more than what people expected.

The first story in this chapter is called the "Transfiguration." In it we see something about the Messiah Jesus that was hidden from the people of his day. People saw him only as an ordinary man who, perhaps, could do extraordinary things. What was hidden was that Jesus was not ordinary at all. If they could have seen underneath the outward appearance, they would have seen the awesome beauty and holiness of God.

1-2. Six days after Jesus spoke to his disciples about his appearing in his glory, he took Peter and James and John up into the heights of a mountain where they could be alone. There as they looked on his appearance was changed. His face shone like the sun, and his clothing became as white as light.

The disciples were undoubtedly getting it by this time that Jesus fulfilled the Old Testament prophecies about the Messiah. They had even come to see Jesus as in some way God; he had done miracles that only God could do. But if we think about it in the flow of the story here, the disciples were still not fully up to speed; they did not quite grasp the whole truth about Jesus. This experience opened their eyes.

3-8. As the disciples looked on, they saw Moses and Elijah speaking with Jesus. Peter, incredulous and stunned, said, "Lord, it is good that we are here. If you wish, I'll build three shelters – one for you, one for Moses, and one for Elijah." While Peter was still speaking a bright cloud surrounded them and a voice came from the cloud saying, "This is my Son, whom I love; I am very pleased with him. Listen to what he says to you."

Elijah and Moses. These men were the two most famous spokesmen for God in the history of Israel. Every Jew held them in highest regard. Their appearance with Jesus demonstrated that he was the one toward whom the Hebrew Scriptures pointed.

But that summary hardly captures this moment or develops the implication of the moment for the disciples. This was as dramatic as Jesus' walking on the water. Who has ever been changed in appearance as Matthew described? And when have men from the past ever appeared? This was either a dream or it was a breaking of eternity into time. And if the latter, what did it mean?

Certainly it meant that something or someone greater than an ordinary man, be he Messiah or more, stood before them. Jesus is at the very least standing as an equal among the elite of Jewish prophets. At the most - and this is what the voice from heaven says - he is above all the prophets. He is standing on the mountain at a moment in time, but he is beyond time. He is God the Son.

It goes without saying, though the voice from heaven makes it clear: Pay attention to him.

When the disciples heard the voice, they were so scared they fell face down on the ground. But Jesus came and touched them and spoke gently to reassure them: "Get up now. You need not fear." When they opened their eyes they saw only Jesus.

9-13. As they came down from the mountain, Jesus strictly told them, "Don't tell anyone what you saw until the Son of Man is raised from the dead."

But the disciples were still confused. They had seen what Jesus could do, and they knew only God could do those things. They had seen Jesus transformed before their eyes. They had heard the voice from heaven. But there was still a prophecy that seemed to stand in the way of Jesus being the Messiah. The prophecy is in Malachi 4:5. Elijah must come first.

Then the three disciples, puzzling over the meaning of what they had seen, asked him, "Why do the teachers of the Hebrew Scriptures say that Elijah must come before the Messiah?"

What the teachers had been saying was an argument that Jesus could not be the Messiah because Elijah had not appeared. Perhaps Matthew's Jewish readers were thinking the same thing.

Jesus explained, "Yes, Elijah does come first, as they say, and will put things right. But I tell you Elijah has already come, and these experts in the Scriptures did not recognize him, rather they mocked him. That is what will happen to the Son of Man. He will suffer in the same way at

their hands." Then the disciples understood that he was talking about John the Baptist.

Jesus answered their question by identifying John the Baptist as the Elijah who had come before him. But it leaves us pondering a second question. Jesus used the future tense to speak about what Elijah will do. That suggests there will be another appearance of Elijah and another coming of the Messiah.

When? Many Bible scholars believe that the two witnesses in Revelation 11 are Elijah and Moses and that their appearance will herald the second coming of Jesus. And what would this Elijah accomplish? His witness to Jesus the Messiah will have such an impact upon the Jews of that future day that thousands will turn to their Messiah. (See Revelation 14 and the 144,000 from the tribes of Israel.)

The next story is about a boy the disciples could not heal. The boy was plagued by an evil spirit. The disciples had attempted to heal the boy and cast out the evil spirit, but they could not. Jesus, of course, did cast out the evil spirit. But he also explained to the disciples that they failed because they lacked faith.

14-21. When they reached the crowd that had gathered around the other disciples at the foot of the mountain, a man rushed to Jesus, knelt before him, and said, "Lord, please have mercy on my son. He suffers terribly from seizures. Often he falls into the fire or the water. I brought him to your disciples, but they could do nothing for him."

Jesus said, speaking to all who stood around, "You have no faith. Your thinking is all wrong. How long must I remain with you to do these things?" Then to the father he said, "Bring the young man here to me."

Jesus commanded the demon to leave the young man, and it obeyed him. And the young man was immediately healed.

His disciples, troubled at their failure, came to him later privately and asked, "Why were we not able to cast out this demon?"

The story brings up the question of faith. How was their thinking wrong?

In answer, Jesus told a small parable about faith to teach them that even a little faith can accomplish big things.

He answered, "Your faith was too small. I tell you, if you have faith no bigger than the seed of a mustard plant, you could say to this mountain, move over there, and it will move. Nothing will be impossible if you have faith. But it is true, this kind of spirit does not come out except you fast and pray with perseverance."

We are perplexed, however, by this statement about faith. It seems so simple. In fact, it seems too simple. Every follower of Jesus knows by experience that we ask and believe God for things that do not happen. So what is the problem? Is Jesus promising more than God will do? Or is the problem something else?

Jesus does not tell us directly. But we can see in the story there was a spiritual battle going on between God and the powers of evil. That battle was not resolved easily. If we are going to engage in the battle, we must expect that it will be hard. We cannot expect to simply speak some canned phrases and all will be well. That is what the fasting and prayer is all about.

Perhaps that is what the disciples missed. They had seen this casting out of demons done so easily by Jesus. They had, in fact, done it themselves when they had gone around to the villages of the Jews proclaiming the message of the Kingdom of God (chapter ten). Did they think it was that easy?

The lesson here is that spiritual conflict demands intense spiritual wrestling.

But Jesus cast out the evil spirit with a word. Yes, and Jesus wrestled with the spiritual powers. He did so in private when he rose early in the morning to pray. He did so constantly as he engaged with these spiritual powers day after day. Prayer was the atmosphere he breathed. He was prayed up. He knew the Father's will, and he commanded according to the Father's will. It was because he had wrestled that he had such authority and could speak the word that commanded the demon to leave this young man.

22-23. Back in Galilee as he and his disciples gathered during a private, quiet moment, Jesus told them again, "The Son of Man will soon be handed over to men who will kill him, but on the third day he will be raised." These words greatly troubled them.

But it didn't trouble them enough. They failed to take what Jesus said as a warning to prepare. If there ever would be a time for spiritual wrestling, would be it. But when we get to that part of the story, we'll find that they had not yet learned. They were not prepared. When Jesus asked them to watch (wrestle) with him in prayer, they slept.

24-27. When they had come to Capernaum, the men who collected the two-drachma Temple tax[1] approached Peter and asked, "Does your teacher pay the Temple tax?" Peter quickly answered, "Yes."

The final story of this chapter reinforced the fact that Jesus was God's Son. The story made the point that Jesus was not an ordinary person. He was not a worshiper at the Temple; he was the one to be worshiped.

When Peter returned to the house where Jesus was, before Peter had a chance to say anything, Jesus said, "Earthly kings collect taxes. But who pays the taxes? Do the king's children? Or do other people? What do you think?"

Peter answered, "Other people pay the taxes."

Jesus went on, "Then the children of the king don't have to pay taxes. But we do not want to cause a scandal over these things. Go to the lake. Cast out a hook and line. The first fish you catch will have a coin in its mouth sufficient for this tax. Take that coin to the tax-collectors and pay the temple tax for both of us."

Jesus wanted his disciples to understand he was God's Son. But it was not yet time for him to declare it to everyone, so Jesus did not make an issue over the tax.

FOOTNOTES

1. The Temple tax was the "ransom for his life" required of every Jewish man according to Exodus 30:11-16. It was an offering of atonement for sin and a remembrance that God had redeemed them from their old life in Egypt. But Jesus had no sin that needed atonement, so he truly did not owe the tax.

Chapter 18

The Greatest in the Kingdom

Jesus and the Little Children, Carl Christian Vogel von Vogelstein, early 1800s.

Jesus had already spoken about the Kingdom of God in chapters five through seven. In those chapters he spoke about the attitudes and conduct of a citizen of the Kingdom of Heaven. He said that God's Kingdom is upside down compared to the way people usually do things. Here in chapter eighteen he added a few more thoughts about that Kingdom. They have to do with relationships between people.

One of the things he added is that someone who belongs to God's Kingdom must be like a child.

> **1-4. While Jesus was traveling through Galilee teaching, his disciples asked him this question: "Who is the greatest in the Kingdom of Heaven?" In reply, Jesus called to a little child - who came willingly to him - and Jesus placed him in the middle of the circle of people gathered around him. "I tell you, unless you turn to me and become like this child, you will not even enter the Kingdom of Heaven. So to answer your question, whoever humbles himself – like this child – is the greatest in the Kingdom of Heaven."**

Now, how is someone in the Kingdom of God like a child?

Here are some ways:

   • A child is not impressed with himself, especially when among adults. He is not proud. He is humble.

   • A child is teachable. He is always eager to learn.

   • A child believes what he hears. He trusts.

> **5. Jesus went on, "And whoever receives any such child who turns to me with the same welcome with which I receive that child, that one welcomes me as well."**

One of the more difficult things for Jewish believers to accept was that non-Jewish believers were equal to themselves and accepted by God purely on the basis of their faith rather than on the basis of their becoming Jews and adopting all the Jewish traditions and rules. Jewish believers just couldn't figure it out. These non-Jews had so many un-Jewish habits.

Matthew included this conversation in his Gospel perhaps in response to that issue. His point: Don't reject or be critical of these new followers of Jesus.

But the problem of not accepting people whom Jesus accepts is not limited to these Jewish believers. It is just as common today. Seasoned Christians complain: These newbies don't know the way we do things. They are not acting or talking like Christians. They are rough around the edges. They are young in the faith.

Yes. But they are eager, and they are learning. Welcome them.

6. Jesus continued, "But whoever causes one of these children who believes in me to falter, for that one, it would be better to have had a heavy millstone tied around his neck and to have been drowned in the sea."

Don't discourage or lead these new followers astray.

In particular, Jesus said that causing one of these children of the Kingdom (he meant anyone who belongs to the Kingdom of God) to sin is very serious. Don't do it. God values them highly.

How might we cause a new believer to sin? We do so when by our example we leave them with the impression that an unholy life, a life that is seriously not like Jesus' life, is okay. God expects every believer to be making progress toward becoming like Jesus. That is called sanctification. If we give the impression that being like Jesus is not important, we can cause others to turn aside from faithful following of Jesus. That is serious - for both of us.

7-9. "It will be terrible for the world, for they cause these who turn to me to falter. Yes, it is necessary for opposition to rise and for temptations to come against the children of the Kingdom, but it will be terrible for those who cause it."

There will be many temptations placed in the path of anyone who follows Jesus. We live in a world that is pagan. The things that our culture approves are often in contradiction to the holy life God is leading us toward. So, we should expect to encounter pressure and temptation to do as everyone else is doing. But we should not be the source of temptation.

"If your hand or foot causes you to stumble, cut it off and throw it away. It is better to enter into the life of the Kingdom of Heaven with one hand or one foot than to be thrown into the eternal fire whole. If your eye causes you to stumble, tear it out. Throw it away. It is better to enter the

life of the Kingdom with one eye than to be thrown into the fire having both eyes."

Jesus did not mean we should literally cut off a hand or tear out our eye. He is using this extreme metaphor to underscore how serious sin is and how serious causing others to sin is.

10-14. Speaking again of these children of the Kingdom, Jesus warned the disciples and others gathered around: "Be careful that you do not look down on these children. I tell you, in heaven the angels who guard them are given that responsibility by my Father in heaven."

To highlight how valuable these children of the Kingdom are to the Father, Jesus told this parable: "What do you think? Even a man who has a hundred sheep, when one of them is missing, doesn't he leave the ninety-nine in the safety of the mountain pasture to search for the one that is missing? And what does he do when he finds his missing sheep? He rejoices over its recovery, more so than over the rest who did not wander away. So here is the lesson in the story: It is not my Father's will that any of these children of the Kingdom should perish."

This parable is often used to teach how passionate God is for saving the sinner. And he is. But in the context of the whole passage the parable really is more about how passionately God guards his children and how valuable they are to him.

In the next teaching, Jesus talked about keeping good relationships with people, especially people in the family of the Kingdom of God.

15-20. Continuing his teaching, Jesus spoke about how to deal with troubles between brothers and sisters in the Kingdom. He said, "If your brother sins against you, go and talk to him alone about it. If he listens and the rift between you is healed, good; you have regained him as a brother. But if you cannot come to an understanding, go again to him and take one or two brothers with you so that they can witness to the complaint and judge between you. That's the proper way to do this, for a complaint is judged, according to the Scripture, by the witness of two or three."

Jesus said to do everything you can to keep your relationship with others good. That means if someone has done or said something to hurt you, go to him and tell him that you were hurt. Hopefully he will realize what he has done and ask you to forgive him. If so, you can be friends again.

However, sometimes that doesn't work. So if that fails take another person with you to help you sort out the problems. Maybe you were wrong. Maybe there was simply a misunderstanding. A third person might have a fresh point of view. Maybe the wisdom another person can bring to your dispute will change the heart.

But even if the person who hurt you is genuinely wrong, having that confirmed by a witness is the right thing to do.

"If your brother refuses to listen to these witnesses, bring the issue before the whole congregation of brothers and sisters. If he refuses the wisdom and judgment of the congregation[1], then regard him as an unbeliever or as one who has left the way of truth."

If going to the one who hurt you and working to resolve the issue doesn't work, then ask the wise and godly people who are part of the community of the Kingdom of God to help you and the person who has hurt you figure out a way to get back together.

If even that attempt at healing the relationship results in a dead end, the community should treat the person who won't agree to work out the problem as someone who doesn't belong to God's Kingdom. He certainly is not acting like it.

But that does not mean to hate them or to continue to be angry at them. It means that you will love them and forgive them and wait for them to change their attitude.

"I tell you the truth, whatever you all decide as the people of the Kingdom will have been the decision also of my Father in heaven [whether it is to declare this man an unbeliever or backslider or to declare him justified]**".**

Jesus taught that the congregation of Jesus followers had authority to discipline a believer who would not follow the collective wisdom of the leaders and the congregation. Paul applied this principle in his letter to the Corinthian church when the church had to deal with an immoral member who would not listen to correction or repent. That man was to be treated as an unbeliever (1 Corinthians 5:1-5). The good news is that when the church followed Paul's instructions the result was the man's repentance. That is always the goal: relationships restored.

"I say this even more strongly; If two witnesses agree on earth about anything they ask, it will be done for them by my Father in heaven. For whenever two or three witnesses judge rightly and judge as I would judge, I am with them."

The one important condition to determining that a person is either one who has turned back from following the truth or is without blame was that the circumstances of the conflict between believers be carefully determined by witnesses who have been involved in trying to resolve the conflict.

By the way, Jesus was talking about resolving personal problems between two people who are believers, not between a believer and someone who is not. But it is certainly wise to do everything we can to solve problems and misunderstandings that may occur between ourselves and others, no matter who they are.

21-35. Then Peter, puzzled about the difficulty of forgiving, came to Jesus and asked, "Master, how many times must I forgive my brother when he sins against me? Is seven times enough?" But Jesus replied, "I tell you not seven, but seventy times seven."

Because forgiveness is hard, Peter asked how many times he should forgive. Is seven times good enough? No, Jesus told him. Forgive him seventy times that much. That means keep on forgiving as long as it takes.

Jesus reminded Peter that this is how God treats us. He forgives when we ask, and he has forgiven us a lot, so we should forgive others. No one can need our forgiveness more than we need God's.

To highlight how important it is to forgive, Jesus told the following parable. He used extremes to make his point, but the point is that not forgiving others when you have been forgiven so much by God carries serious consequences.

And he told this story, "This is how it is in the Kingdom of Heaven. A king wanted to settle the debts his subjects owed him. One of his subjects was brought before him who owed

him the incredible debt of six hundred thousand dollars. [2]

"Of course, he could not pay, so the king ordered him to be sold as a slave, along with his wife and children, and that the price be applied to his debt. At that the king's subject fell on his knees begging him, 'Have patience with me, and I will repay the debt.' Moved with pity for him, the king forgave his debt and set him free."

The amount the man owed the king was exaggerated to emphasize how great the debt was.

"But then this same man who owed the huge debt the king had forgiven went to one of the king's other subjects, a man who owed him a mere four thousand dollars, and seized him by the throat and demanded, 'Pay me what you owe.' So that man fell down before the first man and pleaded, 'Have patience with me, and I will repay the debt.' But he refused to have mercy and had him put in prison until the debt was paid."

The amount the second man owed was not insignificant. It was a large amount, but far smaller than the amount the first man owed the king. Jesus might have made the amount owed by the second man even smaller to make the difference greater, but he did not. He did not because, the truth is, only a significant debt requires forgiving. A dollar could be overlooked. Four thousand dollars could not.

"When other subjects of the king saw what had happened, they were distressed over this harsh treatment and went and told the king. Then the king ordered the first man to appear before him. 'You wicked man!' the king declared. 'I forgave your huge debt because you asked for mercy. Should not you have had mercy on the man who was in debt to you, as I had mercy on you?' The king was angry and had the man jailed until his debt was paid.

"This is how my Father will treat you if you do not sincerely forgive your brother."

The theme of forgiveness is repeated again and again in Matthew. It is fundamental to our living together as brothers and sisters in the Kingdom. And it is fundamental to who God is, for he forgives generously everyone who comes to him.

FOOTNOTES

1. English translations almost all translate the Greek word *ekklesia* used here as church. But the word *ekklesia* is a common word in the Septuagint Greek translation of the Hebrew Scriptures. It means the assembly of God's people. See Deuteronomy 4:10 and many others.

1. In the Greek text this amount is 10,000 talents. Some have estimated that a talent of silver is worth four hundred thousand dollars in today's money. Others estimate the value, based on silver at the current value of ten dollars per ounce, to be six hundred thousand dollars. The point is not the precise amount, however. The point is that the debt was beyond any hope of being paid.

Chapter 19

What Must I Do to Gain the Kingdom?

Christ and the Rich Young Ruler by Heinrich Hofmann, 1889
via Wikimedia Commons

Matthew organized the story of Jesus the Messiah into four parts. The first part is the background of his family, his birth, and his preparation for his work of teaching about the Kingdom, chapters one through four. The second part is his work of teaching and his works of power in Galilee, chapters five through eighteen. The third part is the final week or so which he spent in Jerusalem before his death, concluding in the trial and crucifixion, chapters nineteen through twenty-seven. Finally, there is a short conclusion in chapter twenty-eight, which is the time he spent with his disciples after his resurrection.

This chapter and the next begin the third part of the story as Jesus traveled through Jericho and up to Jerusalem.

1-2. When Jesus had finished teaching in Galilee, he began the journey that would take him to Jerusalem, coming first to the region of Judea on the east side of the Jordan River. There large crowds followed him and he continued to heal the sick as he had done in Galilee.

Jericho. A postcard from late 19th century or early 20th century. Published on Wikipedia Commons

As he made that last journey, he again encountered the religious leaders of the Jewish people. Their opposition to him had grown.

3-9. There also, men from the sect of the Pharisees continued to try to trap Jesus in some dispute that would discredit him.

Divorce was a hot topic of debate in Jesus' day. On one hand, there was the statement in Old Testament that God hated divorce. On the other, there was the example of Moses who allowed divorce.

The last was the position of many of the religious leaders of Jesus' day. But even that policy they misused. They allowed a man to divorce his wife for any reason whatever and, if he chose, to marry a new wife.

These religious leaders used this debate to trap Jesus into arguing for one position against the other.

The Pharisees asked, "Is it lawful for a man to divorce his wife for whatever reason he may choose?"

Jesus answered, "You have read, I am sure, that the one who made man and woman said 'For this reason a man shall leave his father and mother and commit himself to his wife alone, that these two will become one flesh'. So," Jesus continued, "they are no longer two but one. What God joins together man should not separate."

Jesus' simply reminded them of the God's purpose in marriage. It was to be a union of one man and one woman for their lifetime. This kind of marriage, Jesus said, was sacred. And it was God's pattern.

These men were trying to live in the loopholes, the exception to the best that God desired for them. They had found a rule that they believed allowed them to do as they pleased. Jesus brought them up short. He told them that they should not live in the loopholes, but live in the perfect will of God.

The Pharisees then asked, "Why then did Moses allow a man to write out divorce papers and send his wife away just because she displeased him?"

The question the Pharisees asked was a good question. Why, if marriage is intended to be for life, did Moses allow divorce at all?

Jesus' answer was that marriage is to be for life because it reflects God's faithfulness in his relationship to us. It is a small picture of what God is like, and since we are made in his image, we were created to be faithful.

But there is the issue of the hardness of our hearts.

Jesus replied, "It was because of the hardness of your hearts that Moses allowed divorce. From the beginning though, this was not God's purpose. So I tell you, whoever divorces his wife, except for sexual unfaithfulness, and marries another woman commits adultery. And whoever marries a divorced woman commits adultery."

What does hardness of the heart mean?

It means that there are times when the relationship between a husband and wife becomes so strained that it becomes dangerous for one or the other. When no resolution can be found because of the hardness of one toward the other, then for the sake of safety, divorce is allowed. But that is not God's plan.

God's plan is for a husband and wife to remain married and to work together to make their marriage work.

The disciples thought that this was a pretty strict rule. Who would get married, they wondered, if they would have to live by this rule?

10-12. The disciples privately questioned Jesus about this. "If this is true of marriage, is it better not to marry?" But Jesus replied to them, "This thing that I tell you is a hard saying. It is understood only by those to whom God gives understanding: There are men and women who are destined from birth to live the single life. There are also men and women who have been forced into such a life by men. And there are those who have chosen the single life for the sake of the Kingdom of Heaven. Let the one to whom this word is spoken receive it."

Jesus' answer was that God gives the ability to obey him in this - and in every other circumstance. Marriage should not be considered a right by the person who seeks to wholly obey God. God's specific will for a person is what should govern his or her choices. Many missionaries have chosen, for example, to live a single life so they could give themselves fully to the work to which God has called them.

Some homosexuals who wish to follow Jesus, taking this verse as instruction for them, have chosen to live a single life in order to please God. They have not chosen to regard marriage or a "relationship" as their right.

13-15. Then children were brought to him that he might bless them and pray for them. The disciples scolded thepeople for interrupting Jesus with these children, but Jesus said to them, "Let the children come. Don't keep them away, for the Kingdom of Heaven belongs to such as these." And he put his hands on them and blessed them before he left that place.

Did the disciples not learn from the earlier teaching Jesus gave about the place of children in the Kingdom of Heaven? Did they think that it was just an illustrated parable and not to be taken literally? Did they think that they were above what they must have thought to be "herding children to and from Jesus?" We don't know. But in any case Jesus rebuked them for their attitude.

The next story in this chapter is about a man who came to Jesus to ask what he needed to do to receive eternal life.

16-30. As Jesus was going on from there, a man approached him asking, "Teacher, what good work must I do in order to gain eternal life?" Jesus replied to him, "Why do you call me good? Only God is good. But about eternal life, keep the commandments God has given." The man responded, "Which of the commandments?" Jesus said, "Do not commit adultery. Do not steal. Do not lie. Honor your father and mother. Love your neighbor as much as you love yourself."

Jesus answered his question as the man expected. It is what he had learned from the religious teachers: Keep the commandments. At this the man was relieved; he had kept, he thought, all the commandments.

To this the man said, "I have done all these things from the time I was a child. What more do I need to do?"

Jesus replied, "If you want to do everything and be truly a man who pleases God, sell all your possessions. Give the money to the poor, and come and follow me." When the man heard that, he went away in despair, for he had great wealth and could not separate himself from his things.

Perhaps the previous answer about keeping the commandments did not satisfy the man's heart. Perhaps he knew that there was still something he was missing. So he probed a bit further. When he did, Jesus told him to sell all he had and give the money to the poor and come and follow him. It was a test. Had he

really kept all the commandments? His reluctance to do as Jesus said showed that he was breaking the first and greatest commandment, which was to love God above everything else. It showed him his money was more important to him than God.

In the end he chose his money over eternal life.

Be careful. This instruction is specific to the man here in this story. It may or may not be the instruction Jesus would give you or me. We may have other things that are out of line with God's commands, and those would be what Jesus would point to if he were talking to us.

Jesus turned then to his disciples and said, "I tell you the truth, a rich person has great difficulty entering the Kingdom of Heaven. It is easier for a camel to go through the eye of a needle than for the rich to enter the Kingdom of Heaven."[1] When the disciples heard this they reacted in astonishment. "Who can be saved then," they asked. But Jesus looked at them with deep love said, "It is, indeed, impossible for men. But for God all things are possible."

The disciples were astonished because they believed that wealth was one of the marks of God's blessing. If a man was blessed by God with wealth, they reasoned, why would that blessing be a barrier to his entering the Kingdom of God?

Jesus' words were a warning; even God's blessings can become a problem if they are held onto too strongly and prevent us from doing God's will. God gives wealth not to be wasted upon ourselves but to be used to bless others.

The good news is that God can change us, and he can even change our selfishness to generosity.

Peter then spoke up. "Yes! See, we have left everything to follow you." He then asked Jesus, "What reward will we receive?"

Jesus replied, "I tell you the truth, in the world that will be made new, when the Son of Man will sit on his throne glorified so you can see him as he is, you who have followed me will sit on twelve thrones. You will judge the twelve tribes of Israel. And everyone who has left his father or mother or the things he owned to follow me will receive a reward one hundred times as great as what he left behind. And he will receive more, even everlasting life."

The disciples must have felt pretty good about themselves at that point. They had left all to follow Jesus. But there was something more.

"But beware," Jesus continued. "The one who thinks himself first will be the least, and the one who is truly humble will be the first."

Humility. Jesus would have more to say about that later, but here it must have caused the disciples to pause. They, or at least Peter, had just proudly declared that they were not among those who choose riches over following Jesus. Hey, they had left everything. They were among the Kingdom elite, or so they thought. Jesus' warning brought them back to earth. Will they, despite leaving everything, actually be among the least of the Kingdom?

This warning would be equally important for Matthew's Jewish readers. They considered themselves the "chosen people." They were top tier. Non-Jews were second class. Even non-Jews who had converted to Judaism did not have the status of a man born into the family of Abraham. Now God was bringing into the new community of faith, the community called Christian, more and more who are not Jews. Would the same prideful attitude prevent Jewish Christians from fully accepting as equals the many who are not Jews? For a while it did. Jesus' caution that those who think themselves first will be least was as much a message to Matthew's readers as it was to the disciples.

FOOTNOTES

1. There have been many explanations of this metaphor. It is enough to simply say that Jesus was illustrating the difficulty a wealthy person has in surrendering his grip on the things he values to follow Jesus.

Chapter 20
The Servant King

Christ Healing the Blind Man by El Greco, circa 1570.

The disciples had become followers of Jesus as the Messiah early, perhaps as long as three years before this time. But others were believing in him now, as well. So the disciples wondered if they would receive something special that the people who had recently become Jesus' followers would not.

That is the reason for the parable that follows in this chapter.

1-16. In Judea, Jesus continued to teach about the Kingdom of Heaven as he had in Galilee. He again used a parable: "The Kingdom of Heaven is like a farmer who hired laborers to work in his vineyard. In the early morning he went to the market place and hired a group of workers, promising them a denarius [1] for their day of work. Then about nine in the morning, after the first group of men had been hard at work for some time, the farmer saw that there were others standing around in the market place with nothing to do. He hired them as well and promised to pay them a fair wage to work the day in his vineyard. Then at noon and again at three in the afternoon he saw that there were others standing in the market place hoping for work. To each of these men he promised a fair wage if they would work the rest of the day for him.

"Finally, at five in the afternoon he returned to the market place and found still others without work. He said to them, 'Why have you been standing here all day long without work?' They replied, 'Because no one has hired us.' So the farmer told them to go and work the rest of the day in his vineyard.

"When evening came the farmer told the foreman of the crew to call them and give them their pay. He told him to begin with the last hired. When the workers arrived, those who worked only from five to six were given a whole day's pay, one denarius.

"The workers who had worked hard all day in the sun thought they would then receive more. But they were given the same, one denarius. At this they complained to the owner. They said, 'The men you hired last and who worked only one hour were paid the same as you paid us. And we worked all day long!'

"The owner answered one of these men, 'Friend, I paid you just what I promised, a day's wage of one denarius. Wasn't that the price you agreed to work for? So go now. If I choose to give the workers who worked only one hour the same as I gave you, why should you complain? Do you think I am unfair because I am generous?'"

Jesus introduced this parable as a "Kingdom parable." There are several Kingdom parables that will follow in the Gospel. All of them are metaphors intended to picture what the Kingdom of Heaven is like.

In this metaphor the farmer is God and the laborers are those who have been enlisted to work in the vineyard, which is the work of calling people into the Kingdom.

Some of the workers work a full day. Some work only a part of a day. Yet all receive the same reward.

Was that fair? The parable implies that some did not think so. Maybe even the disciples were among those who did not think it fair. But the lesson Jesus taught them was that God is generous to all who serve him. If anything, they should rejoice in the generosity of the farmer.

Jesus then closed this parable with what has become a proverb of the Kingdom:

Jesus concluded, "This is the way it will be in the Kingdom: The last will find themselves blessed, and those who think themselves first in line will be last. Many are called, but few receive the greatest blessing."

This Kingdom proverb, placed here with what will follow next in mind, was a warning not to be competitive, not to seek the highest honor for yourself, or the greatest reward. Seek simply to serve.

Jesus' point that it wasn't about competition may have been perplexing for the disciples. Life doesn't work that way from what they could see. Competition is the name of the game. But it is the principle of Kingdom life that Jesus lived - as the next few verses illustrate. Jesus was not seeking his own honor or reward. He was headed to Jerusalem where he would give his life for us. He was serving with all he had.

17-19. Now as Jesus began the journey toward Jerusalem, he took his disciples aside privately and told them again, "We are now headed to Jerusalem. There the Son of Man will be turned over to the Chief Priest and the lawyers. They will condemn him to death and turn him over to unbelievers to be mocked and beaten and crucified. But on the third day he will rise again."

The disciples, however, still did not get it. But to be fair, this principle of serving with all you have and all you are is so contrary to the way the rest of the world lives that it is hard for us to get our mind around it, as well.

20-23. Then the mother of James and John, the sons of Zebedee, came to him with her sons with a request. Jesus asked, "What do you wish?"

She said to him, "Please allow my two sons to sit with you on your right and left hand when you are crowned as king." But Jesus replied, "You do not understand the seriousness of your request." He spoke to the two disciples now, "Are you able to drink of the cup that I will drink of or be baptized with the same baptism I will undergo?"

Jesus meant were they ready to give their lives as he was going to. Were they willing to face death for the sake of the Kingdom?

They said to him, "We are."

To them Jesus replied, "Yes, you will drink from the same cup and be baptized by the same baptism, but to sit at my right and left hand is not something I can give. It will be given by my Father to those for whom that honor has been reserved."

James and John would, in fact, give their lives. James would die as a martyr not many years in the future. John would live a long life of great dedication and hardship. But they will not be alone. Many will give their lives through the centuries ahead. What about them? Who will it be who receives such an honor of sitting at Jesus' right and left hand?

Jesus did not say. The implication, given the parable at the beginning of the chapter, is that the places of honor will belong to any and all who serve unselfishly and passionately, who are willing to give their life away for the sake of others. For God has reserved highest honor for all of these.

24-28. When the other disciples heard this, they were angry with the two brothers. But Jesus took this opportunity to teach them: "You know that the kings of the world rule with an iron hand, and that the important men of this world exercise great authority. But it must not be so among you. Whoever would be great in the Kingdom, let him be a servant, and whoever would be greatest, let him be your slave. For the Son of Man himself did not come to be served but to serve and to give his life the ransom that will release many from bondage."

Greatness is measured by service, not by power. Power is how the world measures greatness. But in the upside down kingdom, the one who serves others and gives his life away for others without a thought for himself or herself is the greatest.

29-34. Now as they left Jericho, two blind men sat by the side of the road. When they heard that Jesus was passing by they cried out loudly. "Have mercy on us, O Lord," they begged, "you who are the son of David, the Messiah." Hearing them, Jesus stopped and spoke to them, "What do you wish me to do for you?"

They begged, "Lord, Let us see." At their plea Jesus felt pity upon them and reached out and touched their eyes. Immediately they could see, and they got up and followed Jesus.

The chapter ends with what is probably intended by Matthew to be an illustration of what a servant does. Jesus was going through Jericho, the final city on his way to the capital city of Jerusalem. His time was short, and his mind was fixed on the things that will happen in Jerusalem. It is there that he would offer himself to the nation as the King and Messiah. That would seem to be more important than two blind men. (That is what is suggested in Mark's report of this event. See Mark 10:48.) Still he took time to stop and heal these men who sat alongside the road. That is what a servant looks like.

FOOTNOTES
1. A denarius was the typical daily wage of a laborer.

Chapter 21
Your King Comes to You

A contemporary painting in a Medieval Orthodox style.

Jesus and his disciples arrived at Jerusalem on the first day of the week, our Sunday. It was a week that would end with Jesus being accused by the religious leaders of crimes against Rome and finally with his execution.

The week began differently, however. It began with Jesus entering Jerusalem to be crowned as the Messiah King, riding into the city on a young donkey.

Coming into the city riding a donkey seems strange to us, but it was a sign of humility fitting for a Hebrew king. And it also fit a prophecy by Zechariah, a prophecy which the religious leaders could not have overlooked. Clearly Jesus was presenting himself to the nation.

1-10. When Jesus and his disciples got near Jerusalem, at Bethphage close to the Mount of Olives which is on the east of the city, Jesus sent two of the disciples into the village. He said to them, "Go into the village here and you will find a donkey and her colt tied with her. Bring them here to me. If anyone asks what you are doing, tell him that the Master needs them, and he will immediately send them."

This all fulfilled the prophecy spoken by Zechariah: *"Say to my daughter Zion, your king comes to you, humble and riding on a donkey, even on the colt of a donkey."*[1] The disciples did as Jesus said, and they brought the donkey and her colt to him and laid their coats upon them. Then Jesus sat on them.[2]

As they approached Jerusalem a large crowd gathered and spread their coats upon the road. Others cut palm branches and spread them on the road before Jesus. The people in front of him and those behind him shouted, "Hosanna to the Son of David! May he be blessed, who comes in the name of the Lord!"

The crowds were wild with excitement. Believing they were witnessing the coming of the Messiah King, they used words that came from the Old Testament and were clearly words of praise for the Messiah.

But not everyone was convinced.

When Jesus entered Jerusalem in this procession, the whole city was stirred up. "Who is this?" they asked. The

crowds answered, "It is Jesus, the prophet from Nazareth in Galilee."

Most of the people in Jerusalem were still thinking that Jesus was a prophet and as such should be heard and his words considered. But they were not quite onboard with him being Messiah or king. That was a giant step up. But what happened next certainly indicated that he meant business.

11-16. Jesus went straight to the Temple and began to throw out the merchants and their customers, anyone who bought or sold in the Temple. He overturned the tables used for the changing of Roman coins into coins acceptable in the Temple and upset the seats of those who were there selling doves for sacrifice.

He shouted at them, "It is written in the Scriptures, 'My house will be a house for prayer,'[3] but you have made it into a paradise for thieves."

That made the religious leaders angry. Jesus was taking upon himself the authority to say what the Temple was for, and that was authority they believed they had. Not only that, people were praising him, and the religious leaders did not like that either. The people of Jerusalem recognized that there was a shakeup and a showdown coming in which they would have to take sides. It would not be comfortable.

People found Jesus there and brought to him their blind and lame, and he healed them. But the chief priests and experts in the Law saw what was going on and heard the children shouting in the Temple courts, "Hosanna to the Son of David." They were furious. They confronted Jesus. "Do you hear what these children are saying?" they demanded.

"Yes," Jesus answered. "Don't you recall reading that 'from the mouths of babies and young children you have called forth praise'?"[4]

Jesus' answer was a call out to the Pharisees. Would they hear the Scriptures or oppose them? Jesus was not backing down.

17. Then Jesus left the Temple and the city and spent the night in Bethany a few miles away.

18-22. Early the next morning as Jesus and the disciples were returning to Jerusalem, he was hungry. There was a fig tree along the road, but when he drew closer, he found it had no fruit, only leaves. Then he said to the tree, "You will never bear fruit again," and the fig tree immediately withered and died.

When the disciples saw what had happened, they were amazed. "How did the tree dry up so quickly?" they asked.

Jesus replied, "I tell you the truth, if you have faith and do not doubt, you will not only be able to do the same but you will even say to this mountain, be lifted up and thrown into the sea. And it will be done. If you have faith in God you will receive everything you ask from Him."

Many have seen this withering of the fig tree at Jesus' word as not only a demonstration of Jesus' power and a lesson in faith but as a parable. In the metaphor of the parable, the tree stands for Israel. Because Israel had not demonstrated any fruit of faith or obedience to God, the nation was useless. It had the appearance of life, just as the fig tree had leaves, but it was not productive life.

The promise regarding faith is also sometimes considered a parable. The disciples will have authority to cast down the mountain, which in this interpretation is the mighty kingdoms of the world - if they have faith.

Though that reading may be too much of a stretch in interpretation, the disciples and those who would follow in history would have that mission.

The simplest meaning, however, in what Jesus said was that the disciples and we who follow them may ask for big things and expect big things.

23-27. Coming to the Temple, Jesus entered and began to teach. As he taught, he was approached again by the religious leaders and chief priests. "What spiritual authority [5] do you have to do these things?" they demanded. "Who gave you this authority?"

Jesus knew these men were only trying to find some fault in him, something that would discredit him with the people. They didn't expect an answer. It was an accusation that Jesus was taking authority upon himself with no proper authorization from God. He was not a priest or even a trained rabbi. What gave him the right to do what he was doing?

Jesus replied, "I will ask you a question. If you answer, I will tell you what spiritual authority I have to do these things. Tell me, the baptism of John, where did it come from? Did John baptize with the authority of heaven or human authority?"

The religious leaders discussed this among themselves. They reasoned, "If we say that John's authority came from heaven, this man will ask why we did not believe John. If we say that John's authority was merely human, what will the people say, for they consider John a prophet of God?" So they answered Jesus, "We don't know."

Jesus replied to them, "Then I will not tell you by what authority I do these things."

Jesus' answer to their demand was a question that showed up their evil motives. They would not honestly answer his question, and they were not going to obey Jesus even if he demonstrated to them that his authority was from God. They had long ago decided to oppose Jesus, just as they had opposed John.

Jesus then told two parables. Both of them were about the religious leaders. In the first one they are the son who said he would do what his father asked, but did not do it. In the second they are the renters who try to take the vineyard that belongs to the owner (who is God) away from him. They even kill the vineyard owner's son.

28-32. Speaking to them then in a parable, he said: "What do you think? A man had two sons. He came to the first and said, 'Son, go into the vineyard and work today.' The son replied, 'No, I will not.' But later he had a change of heart and went. The father said the same to his second son. That son replied, 'Yes, father.' But he did not go. Which of these," Jesus asked, 'did what the father requested?"

"The first one, they all replied."

Jesus then spoke directly, "I tell you the truth, the tax collectors and prostitutes you revile are entering the Kingdom of Heaven ahead of you. For they believed John the Baptist who came preaching righteousness. But you did not change your hearts, and you refused to believe him."

It was tragic. And it was a strong rebuke. Those who should have been the first to obey God refuse. Those who might have been expected to refuse obeyed.

But Jesus did not leave it there. The next parable is even more caustic.

33-46. Then Jesus said, "Listen to a second parable. There was a farmer who planted a vineyard. He protected it with a fence and built a winepress in it in anticipation of the harvest. He also built a tower for the watchmen who would guard it. Then he leased the field to tenant farmers and left on a trip. When harvest time came, the owner sent a crew to collect the portion of the crop owed to the owner. But the tenants mistreated the crew. They beat some of them and even killed some, stoning them to death.

"Once again the owner sent a crew to collect the grapes, a larger crew than the first. The tenants treated them the same way. Finally the owner sent his son. 'They will respect my son,' he reasoned.

"But when the tenants who had leased the vineyard saw the son, they plotted to kill him. 'This is the heir,' they said. 'Let's kill him and we will have this vineyard for our own.' So they took hold of him and threw him out of the vineyard and killed him.

"When the owner of the vineyard comes," Jesus asked, "what will he do to these tenant farmers?"

They all responded, "He will destroy those wicked men and rent the vineyard to others who will give him his share of the grapes when they are ripe."

The religious leaders who had hoped to catch Jesus in a trap found themselves trapped. They knew they were the farmers in the story. But they could not answer other than they did. It was only reasonable and right. Did they know they were pronouncing their own judgment?

Jesus then replied, "You have read, no doubt, in the Scriptures, *'The rock that the builders rejected has become the foundation stone. This is the Lord's doing, and it is amazing in our eyes.'*[6] Therefore, by God's determination,

the Kingdom of Heaven has been taken away from you and given to those who will do as the owner desires. The one who falls upon this stone will be broken to pieces, and the one upon whom it falls will be crushed to powder."

Jesus told them that God had taken their position as the leaders of Israel away from them. They did not like this - no surprise there - and begin to plan to have Jesus killed.

The riddle of the stone, however, deserves some thought. The stone refers to the foundation stone in the scripture Jesus quoted. Jesus is clearly the foundation stone. But what is falling on the stone mean?

It happens that the word *falls* can have many meanings. The most literal is to stumble and fall. But it also may mean to fall on your face as in worship. That is close to what it means here. Falling in worship requires a brokenness of spirit, a humbling of ourselves to recognize our need and that Jesus is the only answer. The meaning of the stone falling becomes a play on words, for even though this *falls* is the same word as the earlier word, it means, in this case, to fall in judgment. Those who are judged will be crushed under the stone and ground to powder.

The chief priests and religious leaders of the sect of the Pharisees knew that in these parables Jesus was talking about them. They were angered and looked for a way to arrest Jesus, but they were afraid to act because the people thought him a prophet.

FOOTNOTES

1. Zechariah 9: 9

2. Some have argued on the basis of this quote that the author of Matthew did not know the Hebrew language or understand the parallelisms of Hebrew poetry, so he was unlikely to have been the Apostle Matthew. The author must have been someone else, someone who did not understand Hebrew poetry. They point out that the passage in Zechariah should not be read as implying both a donkey and a colt. It is simply an example of Hebrew parallelism in which a single idea is repeated in other words. They also say that riding on both the donkey and the colt at the same time would be an awkward and silly attempt to fulfill this prophecy.

The problem is that Matthew used the Old Testament Scripture in other places with such deep understanding of both the quote and the context that it is impossible to conclude the author knew nothing about the Hebrew Scriptures. The best solution is that a later copyist who did not understand Hebrew poetry but who did know Greek grammar changed the pronouns to fit what he saw as plural antecedents – the donkey and colt.

3. Isaiah 56:7

4. Psalm 8:2

5. The word *authority* in the Greek text of Matthew comes across as "power or right." But this conversation was in Hebrew, and the reference to "right" would have been in Hebrew because it had to do with the authority of God's spokesman. The word would have been *s'mikhah.*

That is what Jesus meant when he asked these men whether John's authority was from heaven. He was asking whether they recognized John's authority as *s'mikhah.* Literally *s'mikhah* means filling of the hands as was done when the oil of anointing was poured out upon the head of a man. It symbolized the passing of heavenly authority to him. The word referred to God given authority.

6. Psalm 118:22,23

Chapter 22
The Messiah Is Tested

The Sacrifical Lamb by Josefa de Ayala (1598-1664)

The inscription to the painting refers to Christ as the Lamb whose death provided salvation.

This symbolism of Christ as a sacrificial lamb who brings salvation comes from the Feast of Passover which was instituted after the Lord saved the people of Israel from slavery in Egypt. The Lord told Israel through Moses to take a lamb and sacrifice it. Its blood was to be brushed over their doors. It would be their protection and salvation during the plague that followed.

Matthew was gradually making the case for Jesus as the Messiah. As he did so he enlarged and deepened his readers' understanding of the Messiah. The Messiah, he revealed, was much more than a prophet and a king. In this chapter and those that follow Messiah Jesus is shown to be the Passover lamb, the Savior.

As the Passover lamb, Jesus was first put on trial in front of the people who were gathered in the temple courts. Later he will stand trial before the priests and leaders of the Jews and then before the Roman governor Pilate. Like the Passover lamb, a lamb that had to be without defect and was to be held under observation for five days (Exodus 12:3-6) so that any defect might be discovered, Jesus was tested for five days prior to the Passover. And in each test he was found to be without defect or fault.

This is how the first test happened.

1-14. Jesus spoke again in a parable. "The Kingdom of Heaven is like a king who put on a wonderful wedding banquet[1] for his son. But when he sent his servants to let the guests know the banquet was ready, they refused to attend. So he sent servants again. 'Tell them,' he said, 'the wedding banquet is ready. The food is on the table. Come to the banquet.' But the guests were not interested. They went back to their farms and businesses and paid no attention to the invitation. In fact, some abused the servants who brought them the king's invitation, even killing some of them".

Jesus was still speaking to the religious leaders and experts in the law who had come to challenge and trap him.

In this parable the king is God. The wedding banquet is the celebration at the end of this present period of history when those who will respond to God's invitation to salvation will gather and the Kingdom will be complete.

The guests represent the people of Israel. For two thousand years - from the time of Abraham - they had been God's chosen people and the first to hear God's invitation.

"The king was enraged. He sent his soldiers to execute the murderers and he set fire to their city. Then he ordered his servants to go invite others. 'The wedding banquet is ready,'

he said. 'But those who were invited are not worthy. Go now to the backroads and byways beyond the city and invite everyone you meet to the wedding banquet.'"

The parable contained not only a warning but a prophecy. The city of the people who had been first invited would be destroyed and they would be killed. That is exactly what happened to Jerusalem forty years later.

But who are the people of the backroads and byways? They were people who had not been originally invited. They can only be the people of other nations.

For Matthew's Jewish readers in the first century this parable might have been almost as much a rebuke as it was to the people to whom Jesus directly spoke. But they needed to hear it. By the time Matthew wrote, the gospel had gone out to the world, and the church was being filled by people of every nation. Jesus' prophecy was being fulfilled. Yet some Jews still considered themselves "the chosen ones." These needed to enlarge their hearts to welcome the non-Jewish believers even as the king welcomed the backroads people to the banquet.

"The servants did as the king commanded. They went out into the countryside and along the backroads and invited everyone they found, the rascals along with the honorable. So the wedding hall filled with guests."

The Pharisees knew Jesus was talking about them in this parable. And the idea that God would choose the rabble who walked the backroads rather than themselves galled them. But that is how it is in the Kingdom of the Messiah. He is interested in the rabble. He has little patience with religious phonies who try to impress him with their religious activities but whose hearts are proud and filled with self-love.

"Now when the king came into the banquet hall he saw a man among the guests who wasn't wearing wedding clothes. He said to him, 'Sir,[2] how did you get into the banquet without wedding clothes?" The man had no answer. Then the king ordered his servants, 'Tie this man up and throw him out into the darkness.' In that place people will cry and grind their teeth. For many are called, but few are chosen."

The man without wedding clothes was a party crasher. He was there improperly dressed by choice. To attend a wedding improperly dressed was an insult to the groom and to the bride and to the host of the wedding. He was not a friend of the king.

This man represents those who take advantage of the invitation but have no love for the king and are unwilling to come on the king's terms.

It is a sobering reminder that we must come to the Lord as he requires: humbly, in sorrow over our sins, willing to turn our lives toward God, and trusting in his mercy provided for us in Jesus for forgiveness.

15. This was the final straw for the religious leaders. They left and began to devise a plan to trap Jesus in his words so they could condemn him.

It was their plan to show the crowds how wrong Jesus was. They would put Jesus on trial.

16-22. As part of their plan, they sent their followers along with some people from Herod to snare Jesus. They said to him, "Teacher, we know you speak the truth and teach the way of God truly. We know you are not swayed by the opinions of others and don't favor one party's idea above another. So tell us. Does the Law of God allow people to pay taxes to Caesar and Rome or not?"

The dilemma they tried to trap Jesus in was one the people of Jerusalem faced every day. They were a subject people. Rome ruled. And Rome collected taxes. But no one liked it. If Jesus sided with Rome, the people would reject him. If he sided with the people, he would be guilty of publicly advocating rebellion. There seemed no right answer.

Jesus, however, knew they were not asking an honest question but were trying to get him to take sides in a political and religious controversy that could only lead to condemnation by either the Jewish religious leaders or those of Herod's group. He replied to them, "You know you are not being honest. But bring me one of the coins you use to pay your taxes." So they produced a Roman denarius. "Whose picture and name are on this coin?" he asked.

"Caesar's." they answered.

"Then Give to Caesar the coin that belongs to him. But give to God what is God's," he said. To this they had no reply and went away.

Jesus' answer was clever. But it also expressed a principle we struggle to put into practice today. What do we owe to our government? Certainly the government requires taxes. But the government asks for more. It asks for loyalty and obedience. Do we owe that?

And what do we owe to God? Ourselves? Our time? Our loyalty and obedience? And what if the two obligations conflict? The answer is not an easy one, but Jesus does give us the principle to apply: Give to God what is his.

23-32. The same day some Sadducees came to him. These men were from a religious group who did not believe in a resurrection of the dead. They posed this question: "Teacher, Moses said, if a man dies without leaving a child, his brother must marry the wife and have children so that his family line is preserved.[3] Now, there were seven brothers in this family. The first man married and then died without a child. His brother married the widow but died also without leaving a child, and the same thing happened to the remaining five bothers. So in the resurrection, of the seven brothers, whose wife will she be, for she was married to all of them?"

Dealing with these conundrums (impossible contradictions) was a regular pastime of the rabbis. But for these Sadducees this was just a game. They did not believe in the resurrection, so the problem they posed did not exist. But Jesus was known as a rabbi, so they thought they'd have a little fun and cause him some discomfort. Probably they were smirking behind their hands. "How could this crude back-country preacher handle a question of this difficulty," they were thinking.

Jesus answered, "Your error is that you are ignorant of the Scriptures and of the power of God. In the resurrection there will be no husbands or wives. People will be like the angels, who do not marry. But as for the dead and whether they will be raised to life, don't you recall what God said to Moses - and to you: 'I am the God of Abraham, the God of Isaac, and the God of Jacob'? Is it not clear that God is not the God of the dead but the God of the living?"

Jesus did not take their question as a joke. His answer was serious. He affirmed absolutely the resurrection of the dead. But he also told them something about the resurrection life they did not understand; it would not include marriage.

Married couples who have lived many good years in love with one another may be disappointed. Singles who have longed for a companion but have not found one may be likewise disappointed. What then will the resurrection life be like if not the companionship of a special loved one?

The best answer is that in the resurrection our focus will be upon God. We will know others, including our mates in life if they are saved. We will love them, for we will love all. We will enjoy them, for we will enjoy all. And we will have forever to enjoy them. But we will have only one favorite, the Lord.

33-40. When the people who had gathered around heard his replies to the Sadducees and Pharisees, they were impressed. But when the men of the Pharisees heard that Jesus had also put to shame the Sadducees, they got together with them to plot against Jesus.

Jesus passed the first test. The people knew it. But the religious leaders were angry.

The Pharisees and Sadducees were usually not on friendly terms with one another. They differed on too many things. But their rejection of Jesus brought them together, and together they represented the stand of the nation against the Messiah Jesus.

How tragic! It could have been otherwise. It was God's desire that it had been otherwise. But God allows us freedom to choose. These men chose to oppose God.

But not all.

One of the men who was an expert in the Scriptures stepped forward to put Jesus to the test one more time. "Teacher," he said, "what is the greatest commandment in the Law?"

Mark also includes this story in his Gospel (Mark 12:28-31). Mark adds that the man approved of Jesus' answer and that Jesus saw in this man an honest, inquiring heart. That suggests there were men among these religious leaders who were still seriously pondering Jesus. They had not yet decided what to do with him and his claim to be Messiah.

Jesus quoted for him, "'*You must love the Lord your God with all your heart and with all your soul and with all your strength.*'[4] This is the greatest command. But the second is similar. '*You must love your neighbor as yourself.*'[5] All of the instruction of God from both the Law and the Prophets is based on these two commandments."

It was the right answer. Every Jew would have agreed. Again Jesus is shown to be without fault.

The Law of the Kingdom of Heaven is very simple: Love God, and love others. If we love and if our actions are governed by that love, every other law will be fulfilled.

41-46. Jesus then turned to the religious men who were standing there and asked them a question about the Scriptures: "Tell me," he said, "about the Messiah, whose son is he?"

"He is David's," they answered.

"Then how is it, "he asked, "that David, who was inspired by the Holy Spirit, calls this Messiah 'Lord?' Didn't David say, '*The Lord said to my Lord, sit at my right hand until I put your enemies under your rule*'?[6]

"If David calls the Messiah 'Lord,' how is he David's son?"

It was now Jesus' turn to question. His question drove to the heart of these men. It had to do with the superiority of the Messiah and it focused on Psalm 110. Is the Messiah a man, David's son? If so there might be room to debate whether this new "Messianic King" is to be received or rejected. But if he is more, if he is the divine Son of God, there can be no debate; either obey him or reject God. It was that serious.

The wording of the Psalm made the issue clear. In Hebrew it reads "Yahweh [God's name] said to Adonai sit at my right hand...." *Adonai* was the title given to God and was the word the Jews used in reference to God. That, along with the context of the verse in Psalm 110, declares that the Messiah was more than a man, more than a king; he was God's divine Son. And he was to be obeyed.

Not one of the men standing there had a word to say in reply; and from that day on, no one dared to ask him another question about the Scriptures.

The questioning was done. Jesus had answered wisely and rightly in every case. He had passed this first test: No fault was found in what he had said. But the religious leaders and leaders of Jerusalem had failed their test. They had the opportunity to acknowledge that Jesus was the Wisdom of God and the Messiah. The truth had been plainly displayed in front of them, but they closed their minds and hearts. Instead of acknowledging him as Messiah they plotted to kill him.

FOOTNOTES

1. A banquet in the culture of Israel and the Middle East was a time of celebration and fellowship. It was more than eating; it was a party. The first reference in Scripture to a banquet celebration at the end of this present period of history is in Isaiah 25:6-8. The religious leaders and those who knew the Scriptures would have recognized the metaphor and would have known that Jesus was referring to the time when the new period of history, the eternal Kingdom, would begin.

What Jesus added was that this banquet would be a wedding banquet with the Son of the King as the honored groom.

2. The word used here is usually translated *friend*. But it is often used in a way that implies a counterfeit friend. That seems to be the meaning here. This man was not a true friend but only appeared to be a friend.

3. Dueteronomy 25:5,6

4. Dueteronomy 6:5

5. Leviticus 19:18

6. Psalm 110:1

Chapter 23
The Day of Opportunity Is Over

Woe unto You, Scribes and Pharisees by James Tissot circa 1894,
via Wikimedia Commons

In this chapter we read Jesus' final word to the nation's religious professionals. [1]

What he says is not pretty; he sounded like an Old Testament prophet. He used the word *disaster*. That means SERIOUS JUDGMENT IS AHEAD. The reason for Jesus' condemnation of them was that they had misled the people. They told the people that the smallest rule was important while by their example they taught that living in a way that truly pleases God was not.

There will be no turning back for these men. Nevertheless, Jesus loved them. In the last few verse of this chapter, Jesus' grief for them was deep.

1-4. Then Jesus turned to the crowds and to his disciples. "The teachers of the Law and the Pharisees," he said, "follow Moses as teachers of the Law of God, so you should carefully follow what they tell you. But be careful not to follow their example because they do not practice what they teach. They pile on instructions about keeping the law, but they themselves do nothing to carry those loads."

The Pharisees and Scripture scholars taught the Hebrew Scriptures accurately. For that reason, Jesus told the people to do what they taught. But the Pharisees didn't follow their own teaching. That is why Jesus called them hypocrites and told the people not to copy their lives.

Where had they gone wrong? They had shifted their focus from true godliness to the appearance of godliness. They wanted to be seen and respected as "super religious," but they had no heart for being truly godly.

5-7. "What they do, they do for others to see and applaud. They make the Scripture boxes they wear on their forehead and arms large and the ceremonial tassels on their robes long. They love the seats of honor at banquets and they desire to sit in the important seats in your religious gathering. They love the title of Rabbi and to be respected as they walk through the marketplaces."

One example Jesus gave was the wearing of Scripture boxes called phylacteries. Moses had told people to bind the words he had spoken to them on their hands and on their foreheads (Deuteronomy 6:8). Moses probably meant this in a metaphorical way rather than literally. It was a way of saying "pay attention to the word of God; make it the guide for your lives." But these religious phonies had taken to wearing a box with a little piece of scripture in it on their hands and foreheads to show how carefully and literally they obeyed Moses. And they had made those boxes big so everyone would notice. But they were not really obeying the intention of the law. The scripture boxes became for these men no more than religious decorations, much like wearing a big cross can be today.

8-12. "But you? You are not to accept the title of Rabbi, for you have but one who is your Teacher, and you are all brothers. Don't call anyone on earth by the honorary title of Father, for you have one Father. He is your Father in heaven. Don't let anyone call you 'Teacher,' for you have a Teacher. He is the Messiah. The greatest among you will be those who serve. For those who promote themselves to places of honor among men will be humbled. And those who seek simply to serve will be the ones who are exalted."

The point Jesus was making is that we should not seek a title of honor like Rabbi. Rather in humility we should remember that each one has his or her place in God's Kingdom, and every place is equally honorable.

Likewise, don't call anyone by the honorary title of Father, for that title belongs to God alone. The sad fact is, however, that Christians began early in the history of the church to honor their teachers and pastors with titles like Father. And today it is a common practice for some Christians to use those titles to honor men. Doing so leads people to think and act as if these men are superior - though they are not. It would be wise for those men to remember that Jesus prized humility and warned against self-promotion.

13-15. Then turning again he spoke these words of judgment: "Disaster is coming upon you, you phony teachers of God's Law and Pharisees! You are shutting people out of the Kingdom of Heaven. You refuse to enter yourselves and you don't allow others to enter.

"Disaster will come upon you, you phony teachers of God's Law and Pharisees! You steal from widows and then go on to proudly make long prayers. You will be doubly damned."

The charge Jesus made against the Pharisees was that they did not protect the weak. In fact, though caring for widows and fatherless children was one of the strongest commands of the prophets, these "super religious" phonies had contempt for the poor. That did not, however, keep the religious professionals from showing off their "devotion to God" by making long prayers where people could see them.

Jesus condemned such phoniness in his sermon on the upside down kingdom in chapter five. But that did not deter these religious professionals. They had not changed.

"Disaster will come upon you, you phony teachers of God's Law and Pharisees! You travel across land and sea to make one convert; and when you make one, you make him a greater child of hell than yourselves.

16-22. "Disaster is coming upon you, you blind guides! You claim, 'If anyone takes an oath by the Temple, he is not bound to keep his word; but if he takes an oath on the gold in the Temple, he must do what he promises.' You blind fools! Which is the more important, the gold or the Temple that makes the gold holy?

"And you say, 'If someone takes an oath on the altar, he is not bound to keep his word; but if he takes an oath on the sacrifice placed on the altar, he must do as he promised.' You blind men! Which is more important, the sacrifice or the altar that makes the sacrifice holy? Get real. Anyone who takes an oath on the altar takes an oath on everything on it. And anyone who takes an oath on the Temple swears both by the Temple and by God who lives in it. And anyone who swears an oath by heaven swears by God's throne and the One who sits upon it."

The charge Jesus made against these men was that they made a big deal about swearing oaths or making a promise more certain by saying, "I swear on the Bible that what I am saying is true." Jesus considered it all foolishness. These oaths and the debate about how to do them "right" made these men appear to be super careful about doing their religion properly. But it was only an appearance. God cares nothing about oaths. He cares about honesty.

23-26. "Disaster is coming upon you, you phony teachers of God's Law and Pharisees. You pay a tithe on the smallest piece of mint, dill, and cumin. But you fail to do the more important things the Law requires - justice, mercy, and faith. You should have done these, without neglecting the

others. **You are blind, and you lead blind men! You strain out the smallest gnat from your cup but swallow camels."**

This charge against these professional religious men was that they were concerned about the small things and failed to do the big things. Justice, mercy, and faith were the big things. What good was dividing up the mint in your tiny herb garden so that you could be sure to give a tenth of the mint as a tithe to the Lord if you were not caring for the poor? Such pretense at devotion was worthless.

> **"Disaster is coming upon you, you phony teachers of God's Law and Pharisees! You clean the outside of the cup and dish, but within they are full of robbery and greed. Blind Pharisee! Do the important thing first. Clean the inside of the cup, and the outside will be clean also."**

This charge was that these Pharisees and experts in the Scripture made sure that they looked religious. But they paid no attention to the fact that inside their real goal was to get rich and live well, even if it meant robbing the poor to do it.

27-28. "Disaster is coming upon you, you phony teachers of God's Law and Pharisees! You are tombs painted white to make them look good, while inside they are filled with rotting bodies and bones. Like the tombs you look good and honest to people who see only the outside. But inside you are phonies and are far from being what God's Law is intended to produce.

29-33. "Disaster is coming upon you, you phony teachers of God's Law and Pharisees! You build elaborate tombs for the prophets and plant flowers around the graves of the righteous men and women of the past, and you say, 'If we had lived in those days, things would have been different. We would never have joined with those who killed the prophets.' But you testify against yourselves when you do in this day what your fathers did. So finish what your fathers started.[2] You are as sly as snakes. How do you hope to escape being condemned to hell?"

The Pharisees testified by their actions that they belonged to the same religious elite of the past by carrying on the outward show of religion while at the same time condemning John the Baptist and Jesus. Jesus held out no hope for them.

34-36. "Look now. I am sending you prophets and wise men and teachers of the Law of God. You will kill some of them and crucify others as criminals. You will have some beaten in your synagogues[3] and you will hunt down others as they flee. So, you will earn condemnation for all the innocent blood that has been shed from the murder of Abel[4] to the murder of Zacharias the son of Barachias, whom you murdered at the entrance of the Temple. Yes, this generation of people will bear the condemnation for all this."

Jesus' final word to these men is a prophecy: When truly wise men and righteous teachers come and prophets stand in the streets of Jerusalem, you will treat them just as the prophets were treated in the past. And what Jesus said came to pass. The book of Acts records their deeds.

The words of this chapter were a strong rebuke to the religious leaders of the nation. They are recorded only in the Gospel of Matthew and were directed toward the Jewish people who were still clinging to the rabbis and Pharisees and priests. They were a call for Matthew's readers to consider carefully the seriousness of the decision they faced: Follow Jesus or suffer the consequences of the judgements spoken to the religious elite.

37-38. "Jerusalem! O Jerusalem![5] You kill the prophets! You stone to death men the Father sends to you! How deeply I wanted to gather your children under my wing as a hen gathers her chicks. But you refused. Therefore, 'The Lord is turning this place into a ruin.'[6] Now you will not have another opportunity until you say, 'Blessed is the one who comes bearing the name Lord.'"[7]

Only a few days earlier as Jesus approached Jerusalem, he had wept for the people and the loss they would suffer for their rejection of God's message and their Messiah. Jesus' tears revealed how deeply he desired that his people would have turned back to God. We can imagine he had the same grief for these men. But after three years of preaching repentance, three years of calling his people to the Kingdom of God, they would not. Rather they had hardened their hearts and plugged their ears. And now there was no way back for them.

This does not mean God turned away from Jews. The first Christians were all Jews, and the early church for several years was made up almost exclusively of Jews. But for the nation, this was the last opportunity.

But the Bible tells us that there will come a time in the future, the time spoken of by Jesus here, when they will say "Blessed is he who comes in the name of the Lord." It will be the time when "all Israel will be saved" (Romans 11:25-32). Salvation will come at last for the people of Israel. But for the present, from this moment recorded here on to the times of the end, God will turn to the nations the Jews had always considered hopeless. The door of salvation will be opened to the nations while the Jews continue in blindness to their Messiah.

FOOTNOTES

1. That Matthew included this episode in which Jesus confronted the Pharisees may be a clue as to the date of his writing the gospel. If he had written after the destruction of the Jewish nation in the Jewish Roman war of 66-73 A.D., this warning about the Pharisees would have been unnecessary. The division of the Jews and the Christians would be complete. But if Matthew was writing in the mid-fifties, it makes perfect sense. It was at that point when the influence of the Pharisees in the church was the strongest and where such a warning would have been most needed.

2. These men represent the religious establishment of Israel, and they are like their ancestors who repeatedly rejected the messages of the prophets whom God sent to turn the nation back to him.

3. Synagogue is a Greek word that means a place of gathering together. It became the name for the religious gathering places of the Jews. There were synagogues in most of the cities of the Mediterranean world and beyond, as far as the Jews had scattered.

4. Abel was murdered by his brother Cain because Abel's sacrifice was accepted by God while Cain's was not. Cain murdered his brother out of jealousy.

5. This sounds similar to Luke 19:41,44. Luke records that Jesus was so in grief for the people of Jerusalem that he wept. His feelings in the Matthew passage could not be less emotional.

6. Jeremiah 22:5. In Jeremiah this is a warning to the leaders of the Jewish nation that they have only one more chance to obey God's command before he brings upon them the armies of Babylon and takes the nation into captivity. As Jesus uses it here speaking to the leaders of the Jewish people standing before him, it is a warning that God will do again what he did in the past, unless they turn from their rejection of the Messiah.

7. Psalm 118:26. As in most of the Old Testament passages quoted by Jesus, the larger context is important. In Psalm 118 this verse follows what appears to be a prophetic description of the crucifixion and resurrection (verse18). As the passage continues, it appears that the final acceptance of Jesus the Messiah is in view. If so, Jesus is saying that the nation of Israel will not have another opportunity to embrace the Messiah until the final days of human history.

Chapter 24

The King's Return

On the *Arch of Titus* in Rome the sack of Jerusalem and the destruction of the temple is celebrated in this relief, circa 82 A.D. The relief depicts the menorah taken from the temple.

The rejection of the Messiah by the religious and national leaders in Jerusalem doomed them. The Temple that had been the center of Jewish life would be destroyed. The nation would be dispersed again in a second exile until the time God had determined for the completion of all things. It was a disaster that would fall upon them within 40 years of the time Jesus spoke these words.

But what about the Messiah King? When will he take the throne to reign? That is the subject of this chapter.

1-2. After these strong words of warning to the Pharisees, Jesus and his disciples left the Temple. As they were leaving, his disciples remarked to Jesus about the beauty of the Temple and its courts. Jesus replied, "These things that you admire, they will be totally destroyed. Not a single stone will be left standing."

3. When they had reached the Mount of Olives a short way out of the city, a place that overlooked the Temple, his disciples asked him privately, "When will this happen? What will be the sign of your arrival[1] as King and of the completion of this time of waiting."

"This Temple will be destroyed," Jesus told his disciples. That was a shock to them. How could this be? Isn't this to be the center of the Kingdom over which Jesus would reign? Maybe it was a metaphor. After all, Jesus had a habit of speaking in metaphors.

The disciples were confused. They were anticipating that Jesus would take the throne very soon, perhaps after a final showdown with the religious leaders. They did not foresee his death and resurrection or a second appearance at a later date. So they asked him to explain as they had asked for explanation of his parables. When would this happen they wanted to know. And since they imagined something as big as this was like turning the whole world upside down, they also asked what to be alert for as this time approached.

Jesus did not answer their question about when. What he did was warn them about the things that will happen before the end of the "time of waiting" comes. Those things included wars and earthquakes and famines and the coming of men who will claim to be the Messiah but are only false messiahs.

4-14. Jesus answered: "Don't allow yourselves to be deceived; many will come claiming to be the Messiah. And many will be fooled by their claims.

"But about the future, you will hear reports of wars and the threats of wars. Don't be afraid. These things will happen, but that won't be the end. Nations and kingdoms will fight each other. There will be famines and earthquakes. But these things are only the preparations for the end."

There will also be tough times ahead, Jesus warned, for those who stand by the Messiah.

"You will be arrested and thrown into prison. Some of you will be killed. People of all nations will hate you because you belong to me. And it will be that even some who identify with you will stumble in their faith and turn back from following me and hate one another. Many false spokesmen for God will rise up and fool people. Lawlessness will become common, and because of that people will turn from loving others to concerns about their own survival. But you, keep on being faithful right to the end. That will be your salvation in the middle of trouble. And then, when the preaching of the Kingdom of Heaven has reached the whole world, the end will come."

This is a general description of the future. These things have been going on for all of history. But there is a climax. The purpose of this time of waiting - the time in which we live - is that the message of the Kingdom of Heaven and the Messiah King would reach all the world. When that happens, the things that follow in the next few verses will happen.

15-28. "But be ready to run when you see the desecration and desolation of the Temple described by the prophet Daniel."[2] (Let the reader understand.) "Then those who are in Judea should run for the mountains. Don't delay. If you are on the housetop relaxing, do not go down and grab things from the house to take with you. If you are working in the field, don't run back to get a jacket. It will be hard for a pregnant woman or a mother with an infant child. Pray that this will not happen in winter or on a Sabbath day."

Jesus spoke this warning about the desolation of the Temple specifically to Jews living in Judea, and he identified this prophecy with the prophecy Daniel had given related to the time of the end of history when things really will be turned upside down.

This event will be the beginning of the most serious hardship the Jews will ever face. That is saying a lot when we know, as we do now, that the Temple would be destroyed along with Jerusalem and hundreds of thousands of Jews would be killed before forty years passed (this happened in 70 A.D) and that in a hundred years those who survived and returned to Jerusalem would once again be exiled and scattered across the world.

The tragedy of the Jewish-Roman war must have felt to the Jews and to Christians in Jerusalem like the world had been turned upside down. (In fact, Christians living in Jerusalem took Jesus' warning to heart and left before the Roman army swept into the city and destroyed it.) And since the Temple was destroyed, it would be easy for them to identify this event as the one Jesus spoke of. But it was not; there is too much that doesn't fit.

It is Daniel's prophecy that the Temple would be destroyed after the Messiah was put to death. There would follow a time of wars. That is the period Jesus spoke of in verses four through fourteen.

After a period of time, according to Daniel, a ruler would come who will make a treaty of protection with Israel. That did not happen in the Jewish Roman war of 68-73 A.D.

Then the treaty will be broken and sacrifice and offering at the Temple will end. This implies that there will be another temple built after the destruction of the Temple the disciples had just visited. It is in that new Temple that the desecration will happen that will cause desolation.

That prophecy by Daniel, linked by Jesus to the period of time he was speaking about, tells us that there is more to come than what happened in 70 A.D. when the Temple was destroyed by the Romans. The book of Revelation, written at least twenty years after the destruction of this temple, affirms that prediction and the desecration and desolation yet to come. [3]

"For on that day there will be great trouble, such as has not happened in the world from the beginning until the present. Nor will there be such a day after this one. If those days of difficulty were not limited by God, no man would survive. But for the sake of those whom God has chosen, he has put a limit on how long this time will continue."

Following the desecration of the Temple there will come a time of trouble described as the most awful the world will ever experience. It would be the final death throes of human history; we would destroy ourselves if God did not intervene. But he does, and he does so for the sake of the people he has marked as his who are living during this period of time. Certainly, many of those people will be Jews, but there will likely be among them, Tribulation Saints, others who have trusted in the Messiah Jesus during the hard times.

"In those days if anyone says to you 'Look, here's the Messiah!' or 'There he is!' don't believe him. For there will be false messiahs and false prophets. They will even do great miracles, so that even the people God has chosen would be in danger of being led astray, if that were possible. But I have warned you ahead of time to prepare you. So, if some say to you the Messiah is out in the desert, do not go out to find him. If they say he is in a secret place, don't believe them. This is how it will be at his coming: It will be as the lightning that lights up the whole sky from east to west."

Verses fifteen through twenty-eight describe the time we call the Great Tribulation. During this time the Jews will be hard pressed. It will be the most awful time they have ever known. And it will be then that they begin again to look desperately to the promise of a Messiah, their national savior.

Into that gap will step many who claim to be that Messiah. But Jesus warned them not to be fooled. Their Messiah will come, but when he does there will be no doubt about who it is. It will be dramatic and climactic.

"Listen to this proverb. 'Wherever there is a dead body, there the vultures gather.'"

The proverb was intended to warn the disciples - and those who would read these words in the future - that people who feed on death will be attracted to the fake messiahs just as vultures are attracted to dead bodies.

29-31. "Following immediately after the difficulty of those days, the sun will be darkened and the moon will not be visible, and the stars will be missing from the heavens, and the spiritual powers of heaven will be shaken.

"Then, and only then, will appear in the heavens the sign of the Son of Man. Then, all the people on earth who have rejected the Son of Man will weep in grief, for they will see him arriving on the clouds of heaven in his power and

glory. Then, he will send his angels who will call the chosen of God from across the whole earth with a call that will sound like a trumpet blast."

After the desecration of the Temple, all hell will break loose - literally. The book of Revelation tells us that Satan will be given, for a brief time, freedom to do his worst, and words fail to describe what will happen. But - this may be one of the biggest *buts* in history - before the judgment of God that will fall on Satan and on the world that has been deceived by him, JESUS WILL RETURN as King and call to himself those who are his chosen people from across the world.

Some have seen in this calling of his chosen people the rapture.[4] It would be good to be cautious about that. These may be Tribulation believers, people who have become believers after the rapture, rather than the church.

It would be fair to ask, however, where we are at this moment in this picture. The answer is that we are in the period of wars and threats of wars and in the time of famines and earthquakes. And what then is the future we have to look forward to if the time of the King's arrival is near? The truth is, Jesus doesn't answer that question for us. We may find answers in other places in the Bible. But in the Gospel of Matthew there is only the instruction to continue in faithfulness to the King until our lives are completed or he returns.

For many people that answer is unsatisfying. We are curious. And if possible we'd like to prepare. But both of those things have proven to be distractions for many Christians. Becoming super occupied with the *when* or the *what* of these things has kept far too many Christians from *doing* what Jesus said was most important.

32-35. "Look at the fig tree. There is a lesson there. When its branches soften and leaves appear, you know that summer is near. Concerning the things of the end, when you see the things I've told you happen, you know that the end is right around the corner. This generation[4] will not pass until all these things have happened. Heaven and earth will indeed pass away, but my words are certain and forever."

Although Jesus did not answer the question about exactly when the King will return (see verse 3), he did tell the disciples that when the things he described here happen, the return of the King is near.

Did he mean for the disciples to expect it in their lifetimes? Some readers have suggested that "this generation" means the people alive at the time Jesus spoke. Since a generation is between forty and seventy years, that would mean that Jesus was wrong. The King did not return in that period of time.

But there is another way to look at "generation."

In most cases "generation" means a group of people having common characteristics, like the millennial generation, or belonging to a common family rather than a specific period of time. Thus it may be a period of time that covers many years and lifetimes. In that case, Jesus was saying that this time of wars and natural disasters and false messiahs will not come to an end before the King comes to take his throne. The increasing frequency of these things will, however, be an indication that the time is coming near.

> **36-44. "But do not ask on what day this will happen, for no one knows, not the angels in heaven nor even the Son of Man. Only the Father knows. For as it was in the days of Noah when before the flood people were eating and drinking, marrying and giving in marriage right up to the moment when Noah entered the ark, in those days when the flood swept them all away, so it will be on the day when the Son of Man makes his royal appearance."**

The exact time, Jesus said, we will not know. Only know that it will happen when no one expects it, when people are going about their lives as if they have nothing to fear. They will have become accustomed to the chaos as if it were the new normal and will not see it as indicating something about to happen.

> **"Two men will be in the field working; one will be saved and the other left. Two women will be preparing food for the next meal; one will be saved and the other left. So stay awake and alert because you do not know when your Lord will come."**

Be ready! Stay alert! That is the point Jesus wants to make to his disciples and to us.

> **"If the homeowner knew when the thief was coming, he would have stayed awake and on guard to protect his home.**

In the same way, as a man forewarned, you must be ready, for you do not know the hour when the Son of Man will come."

Jesus followed his description of the future with several parables meant to emphasize his point of being ready.

45-51. "Who is the faithful servant? He is the who does as the master of the house has commanded him, caring for the house and making sure his fellow servants are fed. That servant is blessed by his master when he returns home and finds all has been done as he commanded. He will be promoted to become the master servant."

The point of this parable is that being ready for the return of the Messiah means being faithful day after day doing what the Messiah left us to do.

"But if that servant does not fulfill his tasks but says to himself my master is delayed somewhere, if he then beats the servants left under his care and goes out eating and drinking with drunkards, when the master of the house returns unexpectedly, the master will have that irresponsible servant punished with the harshest punishment. He will have him thrown into the place where there will be cries and grinding of teeth - where also the religious fakers will be thrown."

There is a warning for those who are not faithful at the task the Master has given them: It is that hell awaits those who are unfaithful.

That makes it sound as if salvation is based on faithfulness. But that is not the point. The unfaithful servant is more than simply unfaithful to his task; he is a traitor. He is not merely neglectful; he becomes the enemy of Master who in this parable represents the Lord.

But if there is a warning for those who serve themselves, there is also a reward for those who remain faithful. What will that be? Jesus explained in the parables that follow.

FOOTNOTES

1. The word used is *parousia*. Though it is usually translated as *coming*, it was used in a more specific sense for the arrival of a king or a "royal visit."

2. Daniel 9:27. Daniel clearly speaks of a time close to the end of history. In the book of Revelation Jesus says that this will be one of the great and fearful acts of the Antichrist. It will mark the turning of the Antichrist against the Jews.

3. Revelation 13:14 speaks of an image that will be set up and worshipped. The time is described as at the beginning of the last half of the seven year tribulation period. The place is not described as the temple, but because of the timing it seems to fit with Daniel's prophecy.

4. The rapture is a term given to being "caught up" to be with the Lord" which is found in 1 Thessalonians 4:17. Christians differ about the time at which this will happen. Some see it happening before the Tribulation, which Jesus is describing in Matthew 24:15-28. Others see it as happening some time in the middle of the Great Tribulation.

If the rapture happens at the beginning of the Tribulation, this passage tells of the gathering of Tribulation saints, those who have become believers during the Tribulation.

4. The word *generation* can mean *race* or a *family* having a particular characteristic. It is in that sense that Jesus meant "generation" in Matthew 17:17, speaking of "this perverse generation." He meant all people who were like those standing before him in unbelief. They all were a perverse generation or family or race. It is also the way Peter meant "generation" in 1 Peter 2:9. "You are a chosen generation [race]. . ." He was speaking of all who were and would be believers in Jesus, not merely those of that particular time period.

Chapter 25

When the King Arrives

Parable of the Wise and Foolish Virgins by Wilhelm von Schadow, 1838-1842.

Jesus continued in this chapter to describe the times at the end of the age in a final three parables. The first:

> **1-13. "In those days at the end of this age, the Kingdom of Heaven will be like ten bridesmaids who took their lamps and went out to meet the bridegroom. Five went unprepared, for they did not take oil for their lamps. Five, however, had taken extra oil for their lamps and were prepared to wait through the night."**

Jesus introduced this series of parables as Kingdom parables - as he had several parables earlier in chapters thirteen and twenty-two. That introduction tells us that he was explaining something about the Kingdom of Heaven or what it means to be a part of the Kingdom. In this parable and those that follow he was telling his disciples what it means to be a true Kingdom citizen.

> **"As the bridegroom was delayed in coming to the wedding feast, they all became drowsy and fell into a slumber. But at midnight someone gave a shout, "The bridegroom is coming! Come out all of you to meet him!' The bridesmaids woke and trimmed their lamps so they shone brightly' The five who had come unprepared found that they did not have enough oil and asked the others, 'Give us some of your oil, for our lamps are going out.' The five who had wisely brought extra oil replied, 'There will not be enough. Go and buy from the dealers oil for yourselves.'"**

The parable is about being prepared for the coming of the bridegroom. Some will be prepared and some will not be. The bridegroom is a picture of Jesus, and the wedding celebration is the wedding feast at the end of the present period of waiting when all who are Kingdom citizens will join the Lord in celebration just as in the parable of the wedding in chapter twenty-two. The bridesmaids are those who are called to the feast very much like the guests who are called to the feast in chapter twenty-two.

The bridesmaids who are prepared are described as having enough oil in their lamps. Those who are not prepared do not have enough oil. Is the oil a symbol for the Holy Spirit? And if it is, does that mean the preparedness of the bridesmaids is the fact that they are "born again?" Some Bible students think so. And that does make sense if we use the teaching about the role of the Holy Spirit in salvation which we find in John 3 and the anointing (usually done with oil) of the Holy Spirit which we find in 2 Corinthians 1:20-22.

But that would require reading back into this parable understanding which the disciples did not seem to have at the time. It is best to simply consider the oil as a mark of preparedness in the same way as the guests invited to the wedding in chapter twenty-two were prepared for the banquet by being clothed appropriately for a wedding, though from the perspective of the complete Word of God that preparedness certainly begins with being truly changed by the Holy Spirit, something that Jesus called in John's Gospel chapter three being "born from above" or "born again."

However, being prepared for the return of Jesus is more than being born again, and even if this parable points to the need to be born again, it should not be read as the full explanation of preparedness. What does preparedness fully mean? Jesus will answer that in the next several parables.

> **"While they were gone to buy oil, the bridegroom arrived and the bridesmaids who were ready went with him into the wedding banquet. And the door was shut. In a little while the other bridesmaids returned and cried out to the groom, 'Sir, Sir, open the door for us.' But he answered, 'I tell you the truth, I do not know who you are.' Be prepared and alert, therefore, for you do not know the day or the hour when the Lord will return."**

This is a serious warning. When the Messiah, the Son of God, returns there will be some who think they are friends of the returning bridegroom. Yet they are unprepared for his return. The consequence is that they are not allowed into the feast.

Matthew's Jewish readers might have considered themselves prepared simply by the fact that they were Jews. Christians may also consider themselves prepared simply by the fact that they are Christians. But as we have seen in the parable of the feast in chapter twenty-two, this is not enough. What is enough? Jesus continued with the next parable.

> **14-30. Then Jesus told them another parable. "At the end of the age it will be like a businessman who has planned a long journey. He was a man having much property and many employees, so he called each of his employees and divided up his property among them to invest while he was gone. He gave each one of his employees property to manage according to their abilities. To one he gave**

$800,000. To another he gave $80,000. To another he gave $40,000. Then he went on his journey."

This too is a Kingdom parable, and it answers the question about what being prepared means.

In this parable there are three men who are employees of a business owner. The businessman represents Jesus. Each of the employees has been given money to invest while the business owner is away. The expectation is that the owner will return and will expect that each of his employees will have made a profit with the money he left with them.

Who are the employees? The disciples might have seen themselves as the employees in this parable. Matthew's Jewish readers might have seen themselves as the employees. We might see ourselves.

What does the money stand for and what is the increase that the business owner expected? The money stands for the opportunity we have to serve the owner faithfully with what he has given us. The increase might be seen as the enlargement of the Kingdom of God.

"The man who received $800,000 invested it and doubled the money. And so did the second. But the man who received $40,000 hid the money in a safe place.

"After many years the businessman returned from his journey and called his employees to settle accounts with them and find what they had gained from investing the money."

The extended absence of the business owner can easily be seen as the time before the return of the King at the end of this time of waiting. Jesus spoke about that time of waiting in chapter twenty-four.

"The man who had received the largest amount came and brought the money he had been given and the money he had made with it - $1,600,000. The business owner commended this employee. 'Good job! You have done well and have been faithful in all I gave you to do. You have been responsible over a small amount; I will now give you greater responsibility. Come and enjoy the profits of your investments with me.'

"The man then called the employee to whom he had given $80,000. This man reported to his employer, 'You gave me $80,000, and I have increased it to $160,000.' His employer said to him, 'Good job! You have done well and have been faithful in all I gave you to do. I am promoting you to greater responsibilities. Come and enjoy the profits of your investments with me.'"

The first two employees made a good return on their investment and were praised for their faithfulness, even though they each earned different amounts. They also were rewarded by a promotion to a place of greater responsibility and invited to join the businessman in his joy over the increase they had made by their investment.

They had not entered into their employment asking "What's in it for me." (Actually in the original language these men are described as servants or slaves. They would not have had a thought to anything but the duty they owed to their master.) They simply did what was expected of them with the resources the owner had given them. The praise and promotion was a surprise - and an honor. The enjoyment they shared with the owner (master) was because they rejoiced in his success. So we will rejoice simply to see the many whom we have led to the Lord.

Often overlooked in the parable is the promise of reward. Jesus didn't explain in any depth what that reward would be. But it has to do with greater responsibility. The Kingdom of Heaven is not retirement to a rocking chair on heaven's front porch.

"Then the employee who had received $40,000 came forward. 'Sir, I knew that you are a man who demands much. You expect to make a profit in a deal in which you made no investment and to earn interest when you haven't put money in the bank. So I was afraid I might lose the money you entrusted me with and I took it and hid it away in a safe place. But here it is, everything that you gave me.'

"'You have been a worthless and lazy employee,' the employer told him. 'You said yourself that I expect to get a profit when I make no investment and earn interest when I have not put money in the bank. You should have at least put my money in the bank where it would have gained interest.'"

The third employee (servant) failed. He did not invest the money, and he made no profit. He did not use the opportunities the owner had given him. The business owner called him worthless.

> "So he ordered that the money be taken from this employee and given to the one who had doubled his money to $1,600,000.
>
> "For in the Kingdom, everyone who has done well will be given more, and he will have a great supply. But the one who has not done anything at all - even what he had to begin with will be taken from him.
>
> "Then the employer commanded, 'throw this worthless man out into the darkness where there will be cries of grief and grinding of teeth.'"

What are we to do with this parable? Does it mean that failure to serve the master will result in not simply the loss of what God has given us but in eternal disaster? It sounds so. But perhaps we should not build an entire theology of salvation on this one story. We need the perspective of the complete Word of God for that.

It would be safe to say, however, that faithful pursuit of the task God has given us with the resources God has given is crucial for every follower of the Messiah. What is the task? It is to enlarge the kingdom by inviting people to be part of it. But there is one more thing. The next parable will provide an answer.

> 31-46. In a final parable Jesus warned, "When the Son of Man returns clothed with his glory with all the angels with him, he will sit as the King on his judgment throne. The peoples of all the nations on earth will be summoned to appear for judgment. The King will separate the people in the same way a shepherd separates the sheep from the goats, placing the sheep on his right and the goats on the left."

This describes the final judgment. No longer is Jesus the Lord disguised in a metaphor; he is described as the Son of Man, the King, and the Judge. This is an awesome and awful moment.

"Then the King will say to those on his right, 'Come. You are blessed by my Father. Yours is the Kingdom that has been prepared for you from the creation of the world. For I was hungry and you fed me. I was thirsty and you gave me cool water to drink. I was homeless and you welcomed me into your home. I had no clothes and you gave me clothes to wear. I was sick and you provided help. I was in prison and you came and cared for me.'"

The sheep and the goats are the people who have lived upon the earth, all the people from the first man and woman to the last. They all fall into one of two groups. The first group receives God the Father's blessing and the Kingdom that has been prepared for them from before the beginning of time.

And what is the reason for this blessing? It is that they have been busy doing what Jesus did, welcoming the homeless, clothing those who were without clothes, and caring for the sick.

Some have spiritualized this. They have made these very concrete and physical things into spiritual things. Welcoming the homeless would be like inviting the lost to the Kingdom of Heaven. But what follows seems to suggest these things should be taken literally.

"Then those who had done right will answer the King: 'Lord, when did we see you hungry and feed you, or thirsty and give you refreshing water to drink? When did we see you as homeless and took you in, or without clothes and clothed you? And when did we see you sick or in prison and came to help?'"

The surprise of those who receive God blessing suggests that what they did was unconscious. They did not think about it. They did not hope to gain by what they did. They just did. What they did was by nature. It was who they were.

"The King will answer them, 'I say to you in truth, as you did these things to the most insignificant of my brothers, so you did it to me.'"

And who are the King's brothers? The King's brothers are all those in need. It is the migrant mother with no home. It is the inner city child with no shoes. It is the displaced man, woman, and children in Africa with no food. It is the man in prison for crimes he has committed. *"Brother"* knows no boundaries of religion or national identity or social status. To Jesus, who entered our world as a man, every human is brother. And the unavoidable point of the story is that what we do for these will identify us as either sheep or goats.

> **"Then the King will say to those on his left, 'Leave my presence. You are cursed. You are doomed to the eternal fire that has been prepared for the devil and his angels. For when I was hungry you gave me nothing to eat. When I was thirsty, you gave me nothing to drink. When I was homeless, you gave me no place to sleep. When I was sick and in prison, you did not care."**

To underscore the point that doing reveals who we are, Jesus described the goats. They are those who do not care for those around them. Their failure to care revealed who they were as much as doing revealed who the first group was.

> **"They will answer him, 'Sir, when did we see you hungry or thirsty or homeless, or sick or in prison and did not come to your help?' The King will answer them, 'I say to you with all soberness, when you did not do these things for the least of my brothers, you did not do them for me.' And these will go off to eternal punishment. But those who have done what God wants will receive eternal life."**

These words are serious and sobering for anyone who takes Jesus at his word. If we put together ALL the truth we find in the Bible about salvation, we know that just doing these things does not earn us eternal life. Trust in the mercy of God shown to us in Jesus the Messiah and turning to God and away from sin are crucial. They are the first steps. But if the one who trusts in God is genuine, that person will then take the commands of God seriously and will take up the task of inviting others to the Kingdom and of relieving the plight of these whom Jesus describes in this parable. We cannot be followers of Jesus if we are not following him in his compassion for the lost or for the least and the hurting of this world.

Chapter 26

A New Agreement

Last Supper by Joan de Joanes, circa 1562. Via Wikimedia Commons.

When God called Abraham to be the father of a new nation and promised to give him a homeland, he made an agreement with Abraham. The agreement was called a covenant, and that covenant was sealed and made certain with the blood of a sacrifice (Genesis 15).

Throughout the book of Matthew, Jesus has been calling people to follow him. He has promised them a new Kingdom. Now, in this chapter the Messiah Jesus establishes a new covenant with his people. Like the covenant with Abraham, this covenant too would be sealed and made certain with the blood of a sacrifice, his own blood.

1-5. When Jesus had finished speaking to the crowds these parables, he said to his disciples, "You know that the Passover is two days away – when the Son of Man will be turned over to the Romans to be crucified."

Passover was one of the most important holy days for the Jews. It celebrated the day when God brought them out of Egypt and into Canaan, the homeland God had promised to them. On that day they became a nation. It was remembered as the day of their national salvation.

That first Passover is recorded in Exodus 12 and happened in about 1450 B.C.. Forever after, the Jews were to celebrate the Passover on the same day of the same month, the 14th day of the month of Nisan (which is our March or April) with a meal of roasted lamb, bread without yeast, and various vegetables. Jews continue to celebrate Passover today. It is that important to them.

In fact, at that very time the Jewish leaders and the chief priests were assembled in the palace of the High Priest, whose name was Caiaphas, scheming how they could arrest Jesus secretly and kill him. "But we cannot do this during the Passover festival," they agreed, "or the people may riot."

The Passover brought many thousands of Jews from all over Judea and from many places in the world to Jerusalem. As many as 200,000 were gathered. And many of these people were hearing of Jesus. Jesus had become a popular preacher and prophet. If the officials were to have arrested him during the festival there truly might have been riots.

6-13. On one evening during that week, in Bethany just outside Jerusalem, Jesus and his disciples were eating dinner in the house of Simon the leper. As they reclined at

the table, a woman came in with a beautiful alabaster jar of very expensive perfume which she poured on Jesus' head.

Pouring this perfume on Jesus' head was an act of great devotion. Matthew did not give the name of the woman, though most think it was Mary the sister of Lazarus, whom Jesus had raised from the dead. The Apostle John, who records this story also in John 12, did include her name.

But Matthew did name Simon. And Matthew named him in such a way as to suggest he - or the story of his healing from leprosy - was well known to Matthew's Jewish readers. It made a connection with them and with the oral accounts of Jesus that had been circulating.

When the disciples saw this they all were irate. "This is waste! Couldn't this perfume have been sold for a lot of money and that money given to the poor?"

This dinner and the pouring of perfume over Jesus are also recorded in the Gospels of Mark and John. In the Gospel of John the writer said it was Judas who complained about the waste. Perhaps it is that John wanted to name the one who started the complaint and who later acted on his displeasure with Jesus by betraying him. In Mark only some of the disciples complained. But in Matthew all the disciples seemed to be troubled. Why the difference? Perhaps Mark, who was not one of the disciples and who was not there, was only recording what had been reported to him, but Matthew as one of the disciples and one who was there remembered that he too got caught up in the grumbling. As he looked back at that moment, he didn't want to shift the blame for the criticism to others. He humbly saw himself as sharing the blame.

Critical complaining is something we are all guilty of at one time or another. It is usually the result of wanting to look good at the expense of others. In this case the disciples wanted to look better or more "spiritual" than the woman who brought the perfume. But they were in such a rush to complain that they did not think deeper.

Their most obvious failure was that they did not wait to hear what Jesus thought. When he did speak, he revealed something the disciples missed: This was a God moment.

Jesus knew what they were talking about and said to them, "Why are you troubling this woman? What she has done for me is a beautiful thing. You will always have the poor to care for, but I will not be with you always. This woman has

poured out her perfume to anoint my body for burial, and I tell you the truth, wherever the good news is preached throughout the world, her act of kindness will be told. And she will be honored."

Perhaps Mary had no idea of the connection between what she did and Jesus' death just days ahead. But then again, maybe she did. Sometimes we get a premonition of what is ahead. Certainly she could have seen the building crisis. Certainly she had heard Jesus speak of his death, as they all had. If this woman was Mary the sister of Lazarus, she had been as close to Jesus as anyone; she had sat at his feet listening to him when everyone else was preoccupied. She might have understood very well what she was doing. If so this moment was a particularly poignant moment for her, a moment of deep compassion and love.

14-16. After this, one of the disciples – the one called Judas Iscariot – went to the chief priests and offered to turn Jesus over to them. "What will you give me," he asked, "if I give you Jesus?" At that they counted out for him thirty pieces of silver[1], and Judas began to watch for an opportunity to hand him over to them.

Why did Judas betray Jesus? Was he disappointed that Jesus was not turning out to be the Messiah he hoped for, the one who would ride into Jerusalem on a white horse and a sword? Was he angry at Jesus' rebuke? Did he see in Jesus' words knowledge that he, Judas, was a thief and an imposter? (This is what John might be implying in his Gospel.) Or had Judas always been in it for himself? Had he always looked at his association with Jesus and the others as an opportunity to benefit personally in some way? And now when it looked as if the end was coming, did he hope to make one last buck out of the deal? We don't know.

What we know from the Scriptures is that what Judas did was part of God's plan. God did not make him evil, but God did put him in such a place where he would play the role prepared for him from the beginning: He would turn Jesus over to the Jewish rulers to be killed.

17-30. On the day before the Festival of Unleavened Bread[2] the disciples came and asked Jesus, "Where do you want to eat the Passover meal that we may make preparations?"

The Passover was both a family celebration, celebrated at home, and a holy day observed by the Jews and centered at the Temple. In Jesus' day a representative from each family would take the lamb he had set aside for this sacrifice and meal to the Temple where it would be slaughtered. The blood would be splashed upon the altar, and then the body of the lamb would be taken home to be roasted and eaten.

But Jerusalem was neither the home of any of the disciples nor of Jesus. They were pilgrims, along with as many as 200,000 others. Finding a place to eat this meal would have been difficult. But Jesus had anticipated that and had made arrangements.

> **Jesus replied, "There is a man in Jerusalem. Go to him and say that the Teacher says the time is near. I will celebrate the Passover with my disciples in your house." The disciples did as Jesus instructed, and they prepared for the Passover.**

The preparations for the Passover would have taken place during the day on the thirteenth day of the month. The Jewish day began at dusk - about six in the evening - so the meal would have taken place on the day prescribed in the Hebrew Scriptures, the fourteenth day.

> **When evening had come and it was time to celebrate the Passover meal, Jesus reclined with the twelve disciples around the table. As they ate, Jesus said to them, "I tell you truly, one of you will betray me." The disciples were troubled at this and each one began to ask him, "Lord, it isn't me, is it?"**

> **Jesus answered them, "The one who dips his hand in the dish with me is the one who will betray me. What has been written will happen to the Son of Man, but it will be terrible for the betrayer. It would have been better if he had never been born."**

Was Judas beyond forgiveness? That is a difficult question to answer. We are inclined to emphasize God's mercy and answer that no one is beyond forgiveness. But Jesus had spoken of the unforgiveable sin in chapter twelve. He had also warned the Pharisees of the dire consequences of their rejection in chapter twenty-three. The implication is that there is a point of no return, a point at which repentance will not happen, and Jesus' words here indicate that Judas would never repent. Judas later regretted his betrayal. He even tried to undo what he had done. His remorse and hopelessness finally drove him to kill himself, but that is different from repentance. Judas never turned to Jesus for forgiveness.

> **Then Judas, who would be the one who would betray Jesus, asked, "Teacher, it isn't me, is it?" And Jesus replied, "You have said."**

"You have said" may be understood not only as something spoken aloud but as something determined in the mind. Jesus was saying to Judas that he knew Judas' decision to betray him had been made; it was done. What a sad terrible choice! All of eternity for Judas hung suspended on this moment. We would have screamed, "Stop!" Would not Jesus have done so? But he did not. He could not take from Judas the freedom to choose. Nor does he take that freedom from us, though our choices might also be choices of eternal consequence.

> **As they ate, Jesus took the unleavened bread used in the Passover meal and blessed[3] it then broke it and gave it to the disciples. "Take this and eat it," he said. "This represents my body."**

The bread eaten at Passover was symbolic. It was known as "the bread of affliction" and reminded the Jews of the suffering the people of Israel experienced in Egypt. When Jesus took the bread and told the disciples that the bread represented his body, he was redirecting the meaning of that symbol to himself. Rather than remembering the affliction Israel had experienced in Egypt, he was saying that he would experience the affliction of their sin. It would be his body which would be broken for them.

> **And he took also the cup of wine and spoke the blessing[4] then passed it to them. "Drink of this, all of you," he said. "For this represents my blood, the blood that seals the covenant and which is shed to take away sins."**

There were four cups of wine used at a Passover meal. (These were not included in the instructions about Passover in Exodus but were added to the Passover celebration some time before the time of Jesus.) They represented the four "I wills" that are recorded in Exodus 6:6-7.

> *Say therefore to the people of Israel, 'I am the LORD, and **I will** bring you out from under the burdens of the Egyptians, and **I will** deliver you from slavery to them, and **I will** redeem you with an outstretched*

*arm and with great acts of judgment. **I will** take you to be my people, and I will be your God, and you shall know that I am the LORD your God, who has brought you out from under the burdens of the Egyptians.* (ESV)

Two cups were taken at the beginning of the meal. This cup Matthew mentioned was, according to Paul in 1 Corinthians 11:25, taken after the meal. It was the third cup and represented redemption.

Again Jesus redirected the meaning to himself as he had done with the bread. Jesus said that in place of representing the redemption of Israel from slavery in Egypt, the cup of wine would now represent forgiveness of sins.

And what about the covenant? Every one of Matthew's Jewish readers would have immediately remembered Jeremiah 31, and in remembering their hearts would have been stirred. In chapter thirty-one Jeremiah writes about the time of renewal and peace for the people of Israel, and he says that the Lord would at that time make a new covenant with his people. That covenant would include the forgiveness of sins and a new beginning.

Jesus' reference to the new covenant would have truly excited these Jews. This wonderful promise (covenant) was specifically for the people of Israel. The coming of this promise was the great hope of every Jew. It would signal the beginning of the Messiah's Kingdom. But when we read about this covenant in the books of 2 Corinthians and Hebrews, we find ourselves included. It is a promise of forgiveness and a new beginning made to all who will receive it.

Beginning in the first chapter and continuing throughout the book, Matthew has presented Jesus as the Messiah. One step at a time, he has unfolded the meaning of the Messiah for his readers: The Messiah is the Son of David; He is the King; He is the prophet; He is the Son of God. Now, as Matthew comes to the climax of his message, he returned to something foreshadowed in chapter one before Jesus was born. This Messiah is the Savior who will take away sins.

A Savior who will take away their sin? If you were hearing this for the first time, this would be a startling and life changing moment. It means that a new agreement has been made between you and God. It is sealed and made certain by the blood Jesus shed on the cross. The agreement is this: With your acceptance of Jesus the Messiah and your commitment to him, you receive the forgiveness of sins! Notice it is the forgiveness of sins, plural. All sins! Sins past, sins present, and sins in the future. All sins by one sacrifice.

For a Jew, who has lived all his life with a deep understanding that his sins place him under God's judgment and only by regular appeals to God's mercy through the sacrifices offered in the Temple can he be forgiven, this word is wonderfully freeing. The Jews understood that the blood of these sacrifices was not sufficient. It was at best temporary and limited; every year another sacrifice must be offered. As the writer of Hebrews will later say, they cannot take away sins - not really (Hebrews 10). But now? The blood Jesus shed on the cross is the final word. The one who places his hands on the head of Jesus, as the sinner placed his hands on the head of the sacrifice in the Temple, has transferred to Jesus all his sins. And in Jesus' death, the debt owed to God because of that sin was paid in full.

"But now," Jesus continued, "I will not drink this Passover cup again with you until we drink new wine in the Kingdom of my Father." When they finished the Passover meal and had sung the hymn, they went out from there to the Mount of Olives a short way beyond the walls of the city.

What about the fourth cup? Jesus did not take that cup or offer it to his disciples. Why? Because it was the cup of restoration. For the Jews, it looked forward to the final restoration of the nation and the Kingdom of Messiah. And that was yet to be. But Jesus said he would yet drink it with them - in that Kingdom. It was a promise that what began here would be completed in the Kingdom. His suffering the punishment for sin and his blood shed to establish the covenant of forgiveness would be completed when they would sit at the banquet in the Kingdom to come. Yes, it would.

31-36. As they were going, Jesus said to them, "Tonight you will all stumble in your faith in me, for it is written, 'I will strike the shepherd dead, and the sheep will be scattered.'[5] But when I am raised, I will go ahead of you to Galilee."

This is the elephant in the room, the thing the disciples had been unwilling to acknowledge or accept: Jesus would die. Now the time had come. It could no longer be ignored.

But how is it that the Messiah would die? Was he not to be King forever? If Jesus died, would not that be the one unanswerable evidence that he was not the Messiah? The rulers of the Jews thought so. His disciples could not even think of it.

Peter protested, "I will never stumble in my faith in you, even if the others do." Jesus said to him, "I am telling you seriously, this night, before the rooster crows, you will three times deny you even know me."

Peter again protested, "Even if I must die, I will never disown you!" And all the disciples said the same.

These words must be among the more famous last words ever spoken: "I will never disown you." But which of the disciples did not? They all ran away. Who among us has not? Who has not seen himself or herself in Peter - so confident of the strength of his commitment to Jesus - and then only hours later denying by our words and actions that we ever knew him?

Matthew did not finish the story of Peter's denial. But John in his Gospel did. In chapter twenty-one John records that Jesus after his resurrection took Peter aside and reminded him of his denial, and then renewed his call to Peter to discipleship: "Feed my sheep," he told Peter.

Every one of us when we fail needs to remember. Jesus forgives even the most serious failures and sin. He never gives up on us.

37-41. When they arrived at the place on the Mount of Olives called Gethsemane, Jesus told his disciples, "Sit here while I go further and pray." But he took with him Peter and the two sons of Zebedee, James and John. Then, overcome with grief and anguish of soul, he said to them, "My soul is heavy with the burden of death. Stay with me and pray."

Going a short way further, he fell prostrate upon the ground and prayed, "My Father, if it would be possible, I pray that this cup I am to drink might pass from me. Yet, may it not be as I want, but as you want."

No place is the humanity of Jesus more vividly displayed than here. Jesus, Messiah, Son of God, the Eternal One, yet human too. So human that he shrinks back in fear at the ordeal ahead.

Yet even here the voice of the Son is heard: "Not as I want, but as you want."

We may never be able to quite comprehend this mystery of the God-Man. But we can see it played out in Jesus' life. We can see something of the tension of those two natures.

Jesus could have drawn back from death. He could have walked away into the darkness and avoided arrest. That would have been the human thing. He could have, but he did not do so. He chose to face the agony of the cross. As a man he chose. He chose God's will over his own.

After a while he returned to the three disciples, but he found them asleep. He said to Peter, "Were you so without strength that you could not stay awake and watch with me for one hour? Be vigilant and pray so that you will not be tempted. The spirit is willing, but the body is weak."

What temptation or trial might the disciples have been prepared for had they prayed? They could not have prayed away this hour when Jesus would be arrested; that was God's will. What they might have done was pray as Jesus prayed; they could have prayed with him that they would have the courage to face that hour and the hours that would follow. God does not always deliver us from sorrow or pain, but he always walks with us through them to strengthen us.

42-46. A second time Jesus went away from them and fell upon the ground and prayed, "My Father, if this cup that is given me to drink cannot pass from me, your will be done." Then he returned to the three disciples, but they were again sleeping.

Was Jesus disappointed? Did he long for the companionship of these men who were his friends? Did he long to strengthen them? Or be strengthened by them? We do not know. But we know that the disciples missed an opportunity to share the burden of his struggle, to confess their devotion to him as Mary had confessed hers. They no doubt later sorrowed that they had not been there with him. Others who have waited with Jesus in prayer through dark hours have found those hours unbelievably precious.

Once again Jesus went away, praying the same words as before.

The place where Jesus and the disciples had gone to pray was the Mount of Olives, which was a about a half mile east of the walls of Jerusalem by path and overlooked the temple. It would have been possible for Jesus to have seen the silent group of soldiers and priests leaving Jerusalem with torches in hand. It must have taken fifteen minutes or more in the dark to reach the Mount of Olives. But Jesus did not wake the disciples until the soldiers were close.

When he returned to the disciples, he said to them, "Are you still sleeping? The time has come for the Son of Man to be betrayed and handed over to the sinful men. Get up! Here comes the one who betrays me."

47-50. Even as he was speaking, Judas, who was one of the twelve disciples, came and with him a crowd of men from the chief priests and leaders of the nation armed with clubs and swords. Now, Judas had arranged with the leaders a signal to let them know which man to arrest: "The man I kiss is the man. Arrest him," he told them. So when the crowd came up to Jesus and the disciples, Judas went straight to Jesus and said, "Greetings, Teacher." And he kissed him.

For Matthew's Jewish readers, Jesus' self-surrender satisfied the puzzle that must have still troubled them: How is it that the Messiah was taken and judged by the leaders of the nation and executed as a criminal by the Romans? Why didn't he fight? That didn't fit with what most expected. The truth that Matthew revealed to them was that Jesus was not taken, he gave himself up to his Father's will.

Jesus said to him, "Sir [6], do what you came to do." Then the Temple guards took him and arrested him.

51-54. At that, one of the men with Jesus [Peter] stepped forward and with a sword slashed at the servant of the High Priest and cut off his ear. But Jesus rebuked him. "Put away your sword," he said. Everyone who takes up the sword will die by the sword. Don't you know that I could ask my Father, and he would send twelve armies of angels. But then, how could the Scriptures be fulfilled that say these things must happen?"

Peter attempted to resist the arrest, drawing the short sword he had with him - perhaps for defense from robbers on the journey from Galilee - and striking the High Priest's servant. But Jesus stopped him from going further. Had he been awake and praying with Jesus, Peter might have come to see, as Jesus saw, that this arrest was part of God's plan, that it was fulfilling what the Hebrew Scriptures said would happen.

But what scripture? Matthew's Jewish readers would have been interested. Matthew - or rather Jesus - did not quote a scripture, but there were many that spoke of the suffering of the Messiah. Among them is Isaiah 53:3. "*He was despised and rejected of men, a man of suffering and acquainted with grief.*" Perhaps Matthew did not quote a specific because they were familiar to his readers. They just needed to be reminded.

55-56. Jesus then spoke to the crowd. "Have you come out with swords and clubs to arrest me as if I were an armed robber? I was teaching in the Temple courts every day this week. Why did you not arrest me then? But this has happened so that all that the prophets have said about me might come to pass. Then, when it appeared that Jesus would not resist, all of the disciples ran for their lives.

Jesus would not allow them to fight. And if they could not fight, what could they do? Their reaction to run was understandable and very human. But it was also part of God's plan. It was ordained by God, for it was God's purpose that his Son face this hour alone.

57-68. The guards who had arrested Jesus took him to the High Priest Caiaphas where all the leaders of the nation and the experts in the Law waited. Peter followed, but at a distance, as far as the entrance of the High Priest's quarters. Then, when the crowd was occupied with Jesus, Peter went inside and sat down with the servants and waited to see what would happen.

Even though Peter had run with the rest, he had not run far. He and another of the disciples, whom John mentions in his Gospel but does not name, followed the clot of soldiers and priests and Jesus right to the High Priest's house where he found a place among the servants in the courtyard. Credit Peter with enough courage and commitment to Jesus to do that.

The Chief Priest and the elders and the council of the seventy, the Sanhedrin[7], seeking to find a legal reason to put him to death, called for witnesses against Jesus. But no firm evidence could be found, even though many obviously false witnesses gave testimony. Finally, two false witnesses

came forward. They said, "This man said, "I am able to tear down the temple of God and in three days rebuild it."

The trial was a sham. But it demonstrated that the nation, represented by the priests, elders, and the council, had already determined to convict Jesus. And they were so determined to convict him that when no evidence could be found they violated the law and called lying witnesses to testify against him.

The irony would not have been lost on Matthew's readers. They were loyal to their nation and naturally inclined to side with the rabbis and Pharisees in their rejection of Messiah and against the growing Christian community. But those men were the ones who stood in disobedience and opposition to God, not Jesus. To follow the Messiah they would need to see that God's path lay with the followers of Jesus rather than the leaders and teachers of the Jews. It was decision time.

The same is true for many, many people around the world today. Following Jesus requires that they break from their culture, their religion, and sometimes their families. What is at stake is life, but the cost can be great.

The High Priest then stood and confronted Jesus. "Do you have nothing to say to these charges?" But Jesus did not make a reply. The High Priest then charged Jesus, "I command you by the living God. Tell us whether you are the Messiah, the Son of God."

Jesus replied to him, "These words are yours. But I say to you that in the future you will see the Son of Man sitting at the right hand of God and coming in the clouds of heaven."

The charge against Jesus was that he claimed to be Messiah the Son of God. His reply could not have been more clear. He declared himself to be the Son of Man and he connected that claim with Daniel 7:13, 14. It left no room for doubt:

*In my vision at night I looked, and there before me was one like a **son of man**, coming with the clouds of heaven. He approached the Ancient of Days and was led into his presence. He was given authority, glory and sovereign power; all nations and peoples of every language worshiped him. His dominion is an everlasting dominion that will not pass away, and his Kingdom is one that will never be destroyed.* (Daniel 7:13-14, emphasis is mine)

It is significant that Matthew alone of all the Gospel writers included this reply to the High Priest. Matthew's purpose was to argue before a Jewish audience that Jesus was the Messiah. But Jesus throughout his teaching ministry avoided making that claim in an unequivocal way. That would have focused the hatred of the religious leaders upon him too early. He rather allowed what he did to speak for him. However, at this point it was time to be clear. Matthew's inclusion of this reply again puts every Jewish reader at the point of decision. There can be no riding the fence. Either they believed Jesus and worshiped him or they rejected him and agreed with his condemnation.

At Jesus' words, the Chief Priest tore his robes [an act of extreme condemnation] and said, "What more do we need to hear? He has spoken in contempt of God Almighty. We need no witnesses. We have heard it ourselves. What is your judgment?"

Jesus would have been guilty of blasphemy (of elevating himself to the position of the Son of God), as the High Priest declared, IF it were not true. But for three years Jesus had demonstrated to them and to the Jewish nation that it was true. He was the Son of God, the Messiah. He was not guilty.

We cannot know whether or not the High Priest condemned Jesus fully knowing that he was condemning the Messiah. Human nature as it is, we can tell ourselves convenient lies. We can even come to believe them. But it seems like the High Priest and all the others, knowingly and for their own purposes, condemned the man they knew to be the Messiah. To knowingly do so and by doing so to condemn yourself before God is so extremely rash it is shocking. But how many others make similar choices, and by those choices miss eternal life?

They all answered, "He is guilty of death." Then they spit in his face and struck him with their open hands. They contemptuously demanded of him, "Tell us, you who call yourself Messiah, who struck you?"

69-75. While this was going on inside, Peter sat in the courtyard. A young servant girl came by and looking at him said, "You! You were with Jesus in Galilee." But Peter strongly denied it in front of everyone there. "I don't know what you are talking about," he said.

These two events, the condemnation of Jesus and Peter's denial, juxtaposed as they were by Matthew, contrast Jesus' love in the face of both hatred by his enemies and denial by his friends. Jesus chose this path, knowing the cost, for the sake of these very men who hated him and for those who denied him. And for us, for it was for all of us that he died..

Getting up from there Peter went out to the entrance and another girl saw him and said, "You were one of those with Jesus of Nazareth." And Peter again firmly denied it. "I do not know this man!" A short while later some others standing around noticed Peter and said to him, "You must be one of the disciples of this man – you sound like a Galilean." And again Peter vehemently denied it with an oath, "I do not know this man." Immediately, the rooster crowed. Peter remembered that Jesus had said "before the rooster crows, you will deny me three times," and he left the place crying bitterly.

Jesus' prophecy about Peter came to pass. But Peter was not the only one to deny his association with Jesus. All the disciples ran away at his arrest. All were hiding, except Peter and the unnamed disciple. All failed to stand with him. And that would have included Matthew, the author of this Gospel. Peter, at least, wept over his failure.

And what was Matthew's purpose in showing Peter's denial? Remember Matthew was not randomly including things in this story. He has a purpose. One purpose might be to show how utterly abandoned Jesus was as he walked the path God had placed before him and how even this fits the prophecy of Zechariah: "*Strike the shepherd and the sheep will be scattered.*"

It was the scripture quoted by Jesus in verse thirty-one. And like almost every scripture quoted, the whole passage was significant; it predicted destruction of the whole land of Israel. Two-thirds of the inhabitants would die. And they did just forty years later.

FOOTNOTES

1. The thirty pieces of silver recalls Zechariah 11:12. If the money the chief priests gave to Judas was literally thirty piece of silver, it would have been hugely ironic. They knew this passage in Zechariah. They knew that it was a scathing rebuke of the leaders of the nation. It is unlikely that the priests would have knowingly done something that implicated them as the shepherds of the flock doomed to slaughter. It is more likely that this is metaphorical. It was Matthew's message to his readers that the chief priests in paying Judas to betray Jesus rejected the Lord's Shepherd, as pictured in Zechariah, and would suffer the consequences – the covenant of God with the nation would be broken.

If, however, the priests did give Judas thirty pieces of silver knowing the passage in Zechariah, if would have been the ultimate rejection by men whose faith had long since crumbled to dust. They just did not care.

If Matthew wrote this prior to the war with Rome in which the Temple and Jerusalem were destroyed, what is spoken of in Zechariah was very soon to happen. The shepherds of Israel, who were the priests, would be no more.

2. Most translations call this the first day of the festival. That would have been the fourteenth day of the month of Nisan, which was the day of the Passover. But the word "day" is not in the Greek text. Literally the verse reads "The first of the unleavened" or "Just before the unleavened." The context suggests that it is the day before the Passover, which was in Jesus' time considered to be the beginning of the Feast of Unleavened Bread. That means that this day was the 13th of the month of Nisan. The way Matthew described this is particularly Jewish

3. The traditional blessing is "Praised are you, Adonai our God, Ruler of the universe, who brings bread from out of the earth."

4. The traditional blessing of the wine is "Praise to You, Eternal, our God, Sovereign of the Universe, Creator of the fruit of the vine."

5. Zechariah 13:7. This passage goes on to predict the punishment of those who reject the shepherd. Two-thirds will perish, but when the rest have been brought through the fire they will call on the name of the Lord and he will save them.

6. Literally the word used here is translated "friend," but it is used to address a false friend rather than a genuine friend.

7. The Great Sanhedrin was made up of sixty-nine men plus a Chief Justice. The High Priest also had a vote so that there could be no split decisions. It was the high court of the Jewish nation.

Chapter 27
Death and Resurrection

Ecce homo by Antonio Ciseri, circa 1880

A Jewish explanation of the things recorded in this chapter by Matthew is found in the Babylonian Talmud, a collection of writings explaining and applying the Hebrew Law. The Babylonian Talmud explained that Jesus (Yeshu, a short mocking form of the name Jesus) was condemned to death for sorcery and for leading the Jews away from God and into apostasy. These were Jewish religious crimes, and the Talmud says that Yeshu was condemned to death by stoning, the Jewish method of death for a religious crime. But the Talmud indicates Yeshu was not stoned. Rather he was hanged (crucified). Why? In this chapter Matthew tells the story the way it happened. And he explains why.

In Matthew twenty-seven the author connects Jesus' death to Psalm 22 where the death of the Messiah is described prophetically in greater detail than in any other place. Some of those are:

Psalm 22:7,8. *But I am a worm and not a man, scorned by everyone, despised by the people. All who see me mock me; they hurl insults, shaking their heads. "He trusts in the Lord," they say, "let the Lord rescue him. Let him deliver him, since he delights in him."* (He is mocked.)

Psalm 22:12,13. *Many bulls surround me; strong bulls of Bashan encircle me. Roaring lions that tear their prey open their mouths wide against me.* (He is surrounded by his enemies.)

Psalm 22:15. *My mouth is dried up like a potsherd, and my tongue sticks to the roof of my mouth; you lay me in the dust of death.* (That is why the soldiers offered him a sponge of wine and vinegar.)

It is clear by the last verses of Psalm 22 that it pictures crucifixion. Matthew included the details he did to show that Jesus' death fit the picture.

1-2. Early in the morning the chief priests and the leaders of the people made plans how to put Jesus to death. Their plan was to bring him to the Roman governor Pilate, so they bound him as a criminal and handed him over to the governor.

Matthew did not include in his account that Pilate sent Jesus to Herod. Luke provided that detail. It was not something that fit Matthew's purpose in his Gospel; he wanted to show how the trial and the execution of Jesus fit the prophecies in the Hebrew Scriptures and how the Jewish leaders pressed for his crucifixion. The part about Herod's involvement was unnecessary detail.

3-10. When Judas saw that Jesus had been condemned by the priests and Sanhedrin he was crushed with remorse, and he brought back the thirty pieces of silver he had received for betraying Jesus. "I sinned," he said, "in betraying an innocent man."

"What do we care?" the priests replied. "That is your responsibility." So Judas threw the money back at them, and he left the temple and hanged himself.

Of the gospel writers, only Matthew included this part of the story, though Luke in the book of Acts referred to it. Matthew's purpose was to show that even Judas recognized Jesus was innocent and to show that the nation's leaders, the priests and Sanhedrin, were so determined to get rid of Jesus that they did not care about what was just or true.

In doing so Matthew pressed his Jewish readers to the decision point. If Jesus was innocent, if he was the Messiah, if he was the Son of God - and all the evidence Matthew has provided said that he was - then to side with the nation's leaders against the Messiah is to choose a lie over the truth. It is to side with men against God, and ultimately every Jew knew that was a death sentence.

It was a very real dilemma for the mid-first century Jews to whom Matthew wrote. Luke in Acts describes the scene in the mid-first century. Not only are the Jews in Jerusalem stepping up their attacks on the new community of Jesus followers but Jews around the Roman world are taking sides. If a Jew were to become a follower of Jesus it would mean persecution, expulsion from the synagogue and the Jewish community, and rejection by his family. He would be hated and despised. It was a life altering decision. The only possible reason for making the decision to follow Jesus was that it was true: Jesus was the Messiah.

Most of us are not faced with quite as stark a choice, but we all are faced with the choice between falsehood and truth and ultimately between pleasing men or pleasing God. There is absolutely no reason good enough to become a follower of Jesus except the truth that he was and is the Son of God, the Messiah.

The chief priests picked up the coins but said, "We can't return this to the treasury. It is unclean because it was used to bring about death." So they bought a field, called the Potter's Field, to be used as a cemetery for foreigners. From that time on, it has been called the Field of Blood. In that,

the prophecy of Jeremiah [and of Zechariah] came to pass.
***"They used the thirty pieces of silver, which was the value
set upon him by the men of Israel, and they bought the
Potter's Field, as the Lord commanded me."***

Luke's account in Acts of the purchase of this field and the death of Judas differs from Matthew's. In Acts **Judas** bought the field; in Matthew the **priests** bought the field. In Acts Judas **fell and his body burst open**; In Matthew **he hanged himself**.

Skeptics have made a big deal of what they call a "conflict." For them it is evidence that the Scripture is neither reliably true nor inspired by God. Can the conflict be resolved?

There have been many suggestions how the two accounts can be reconciled (made to fit together). If you check the Internet, there are so many that the explanations are themselves confusing. Most of those explanations depend on a careful analysis of the grammar and words. A better approach to the question might be a rhetorical analysis. (*Rhetorical* means the way the author used details in his story to achieve the effect he wanted.) When the question "why are they different" is answered the two accounts agree.

Matthew's rhetorical purpose was to show how the story of Judas fit prophecy. That is what his Jewish audience would be interested in. So he referred to the prophecies of Jeremiah and Zechariah, and he included in his Gospel the details that related to the prophecies.

How did Matthew relate the prophets to this event? First, he connected Jeremiah, using his name but not a direct quote, to the Potter's Field. In Jeremiah 19, Jeremiah bought a clay pot from a potter's house and took the leaders of Jerusalem with him to the valley of Ben Hinnom, a place where formerly there had been human sacrifices to the god Molech. It was, therefore, a cursed place, the most unclean place in Jerusalem (just outside the city actually). He broke the pot there and told these men this would be where they too would come to their end. And they did just a few years later. That place became known as the "Potter's Field."

The prophecy of Zechariah 11:12 and 13 Matthew referred to was given almost one hundred years after Jeremiah's. It refers to a future day when the people of Israel will be oppressed by their leaders (the worthless shepherds) and when God will send a man who will be a faithful shepherd for the people. The people, the prophet predicts, will reject the faithful shepherd, and God will cancel the covenant of favor he made with them.

The faithful shepherd asks them - with strong tones of sarcasm - what they will pay him for his services as their shepherd, and they pay him the insulting price of thirty pieces of silver. He then takes that payment and throws it into the house of the Lord to the "potter". (The word *potter* means maker or doer. It refers in Zechariah to the worthless shepherds.) The priests - the doers - are the ones charged by God with caring for the people, but they turn against him. The Faithful shepherd rejects their mocking payment given for his services. And he rejects them.

Zechariah's prophecy pictures what happened when the present Jews and their leaders rejected the Messiah Jesus: They are rejected by God and the covenant with them canceled. The two prophecies are linked to these present priests by the fact that the thirty pieces of silver Judas threw back into the temple were used by the priests to buy the "Potter's Field."

With that, the two pieces of the prophetic puzzle come together. The purchase of the Potter's Field with the thirty pieces of silver would have been immediately recognized by Jewish readers as a chilling irony. The "Potter's Field" was cursed. The priests owned that field. Owning the field, they owned the curse and their own destruction.

The link between Jeremiah and Zechariah may seem difficult to follow. But it would have been perfectly and powerfully clear to the Jewish mind. It was the manner of teaching used by the rabbis.

Matthew's purpose was to double underline how the leaders of the nation insulted the Messiah Jesus by the value they placed on him in the price they paid Judas for his betrayal. That is why Matthew included the details and the prophecies. But his purpose is also to point out the irony: The present priests bought for themselves the curse. That irony would play out in a dramatic way just forty years later when these priests would meet their end in the Roman destruction of Jerusalem. They would be broken pots, just as the pots Jeremiah used to symbolize the destruction of the priests in his day. Indeed, when the Romans destroyed Jerusalem and the temple in 70 A.D., the priesthood came to an end. From that moment on, the leaders of the Jews would be the rabbis, not the priests.

Luke's purpose in Acts was far more simple. He merely wants to show how Judas' life ended and how he was replaced by another man as an apostle. He does not want to dwell on Judas or the priests. Consequently, he condenses the story. He skips the role of the priests and attributes the buying of the field to Judas; it was his money, after all, that went to purchase the field.

Because Matthew and Luke had different purposes in writing, their accounts included different details.

Regarding the differences between the descriptions of Judas' death, they can be reconciled in this way. Sometime after Judas returned the money to the priests he hanged himself. How long after we don't know. It may not have been immediately. But it apparently was long enough for the priests to have purchased the field.

His body quickly bloated by the gases of decomposition in the heat of the day. Soon the body ballooned to the place that if it were punctured the intestines would explode outward. And that is what Luke describes.

When did that happen? We don't know. It might have been when his body was cut down from the tree or other overhang from which he had hanged himself. It may have been that eventually the noose that was around his neck gave way and the body fell. In any event, when the body fell, it burst open. So he both hanged himself and the body burst open.

Where did it happen? It happened at the field the priests had purchased with Judas' money. The field was intended by them to be a cemetery for foreigners because it was a place cursed by the sacrifices given to Molech centuries earlier. It was unsuitable for anything else. Ironically, Judas by his betrayal of the Messiah made himself both a foreigner and a curse.

One final puzzle: Why did Matthew cite Jeremiah as the source of the prophecy rather than Zechariah, or why did he not cite both? The answer is that Zechariah's reference to the potter and the thirty pieces of silver completed the prophecy of Jeremiah; it extended the prophecy of the destruction of the leaders of Jerusalem to point not to the leaders of Jerusalem before the destruction of Jerusalem by the Babylonians but to leaders who would come later. The two prophets wrote about the same topic: the "false shepherds" of Jesus' day who paid the thirty pieces of silver to Judas. Jewish readers would have immediately recognized Zechariah as the source of the quote. The reference to Jeremiah was all that was needed to make the link between the two.

11-23. As all this was happening, Jesus was standing as an accused criminal before Pilate. The governor asked him, "Are you the King of the Jews?"

This all looked to Pilate like a meaningless religious squabble, so the Jews made their accusation political. Luke explains: The Jews argued that because

Jesus claimed to be a king and because he was a rebel Caesar would be displeased if Pilate did not execute him.

Only this charge would have gotten Pilate's attention. Pilate was unwilling to risk Caesar's displeasure. It did not matter if Jesus was guilty or not. If Caesar heard that he had not executed a rebel king it would have been disaster for Pilate. What was the death of one obscure Jew?

Jesus replied, "Those words are yours." But when the chief priests and leaders of the Jews brought their charges against, he did not reply.

"Don't you hear what they are saying about you?" Pilate asked. Still Jesus did not reply, not even to a single accusation. At that the governor was perplexed.

This was unusual. Jesus was unusual, even noble; he refused to respond to the accusations. Pilate expected Jesus to put up a defense; every criminal has some defense or excuse. There was something different going on here. Pilate was troubled.

Now it happened that the governor had as a gesture of good will a custom at the festival of releasing a Jew who had been condemned for a crime. There was at the time a well-known criminal named Barabbas. So when a crowd had gathered, Pilate called out to them, "Which of these men would you have me release? Barabbas or Jesus called the Messiah?" (He knew that it was purely out of a personal vendetta that they had brought Jesus to him and not because of a serious crime.)

Pilate was still not convinced that Jesus was guilty of what the Jews claimed. He thought this was just a mob that had gotten out of control and would calm down if given the chance. Maybe just making their point that Jesus was trouble would satisfy them. Maybe they would accept that he had suffered enough. Maybe they would take the way out Pilate offered.

While he waited, sitting on the judge's seat, his wife sent him a message: "Don't get involved with this man. He is innocent, and I had a nightmare last night about him." But the chief priests and the Jewish leaders, meanwhile, had

talked the crowd into asking that Barabbas be released and that Jesus be executed.

Dreams were a big deal for people in those days. They believed strongly in omens and portents. When Pilate's wife warned him of her dream, he was spooked. But he still was the Roman governor. He had to make a choice.

When it was time for a decision, Pilate asked, "Which of these two do you want me to set free?"

"Barabbas," the crowd answered.

"What do you want me to do to Jesus who is called the Anointed?" Pilate asked. The crowd shouted, "Crucify him!"

"Why? What crime has he committed?

Pilate found Jesus guilty of no crime. Earlier, the priests and Sanhedrin had found him guilty of no crime - for Jesus was in fact the Son of God, and it was no crime for him to declare that so. So ends the trial of Jesus before the people, before the religious leaders, and before Pilate. He was found to be without fault and, like the lamb sacrificed at Passover, qualified to bear the sins of the people.

But the crowd shouted even more loudly, "Crucify him!"

24-26. Pilate saw that he could not change the mind of the people and that there was danger of a riot, so he had a basin of water brought, and he washed his hands in it. "My hands are clean of this man's blood," he told the crowd. "It is your responsibility."

It is difficult to believe that Pilate would be so easily convinced to do what the Jews wanted. He was known for being a harsh man, and the Jews were not his friends. He had more of an issue with them than with Jesus, whom he saw as a misguided but harmless preacher. So why did Pilate give the Jews what they wanted? Because the Jews accused Jesus of crimes against Rome (John 19:11-13). Pilate could not overlook that because if report that he allow a rebel to go free reached Tiberius, the Roman emperor, he would be in trouble. That is how a man who might have been condemned by the Jews and executed for religious crimes by stoning came to be executed by the Romans by crucifixion. But in his crucifixion the predictions of the Old Testament regarding the Messiah came to pass.

See Isaiah 53:5 and Psalm 22:16. Even in his death, Jesus is shown to be the Messiah.

The crowd shouted back, "Let his blood be upon us and upon our children!" So Pilate released Barabbas and ordered Jesus beaten and then handed him over to the crowd to be put to death.

Jesus was despised. Psalm 22:6. *"But I am a worm and not a man, scorned by everyone, despised by the people."*

27-31. The governor's soldiers took Jesus into the headquarters building and a whole company gathered around him. They stripped off his clothes and put a red robe on him. Then they twisted a branch from a thorn tree into a rude crown and placed it on his head. They put a staff in his right hand, and bowed before him mocking him. "Hail, King of the Jews!" Then they spit on him and struck him repeatedly on the head with the staff. When they had finished with their fun, they put his own clothes back on him and led him out to be put to death.

Jesus was mocked. Psalm 22:7. *"All who see me mock me; they hurl insults, shaking their heads."*

32-44. Along the way they came upon a man named Simon from Cyrene, and they made him carry Jesus' cross. When they had come to the hill called Golgotha (which is also called the place of the skull because it has the appearance of a skull), they offered Jesus a drink of wine and gall, which would dull his pain, but he tasted it and refused it.

After they nailed Jesus to the cross, they divided up his clothing, casting lots for his shirt. Then the soldiers sat down to wait as he died. Above his head they placed the written notice of his crimes: THIS IS JESUS, KING OF THE JEWS.

Not all who were crucified were nailed to the cross. In fact, it was unusual and until recently was a detail that could not be confirmed by archaeology, though it is described by the Jewish historian Josephus.

Matthew described Jesus' crucifixion and said he was nailed to the cross. And Psalm 22:16 points to nails that pierced the hands and feet: "*Dogs surround me, a pack of villains encircles me; they pierce my hands and my feet.*"

Regarding the casting of lost for his clothes, that is in Psalm 22:18. "*They divide my clothes among them and cast lots for my garment.*"

On each side two rebels were also crucified. People who passed by going to or from the city shouted insults at Jesus. "So you were going to tear down the Temple and rebuild it in three days? So, save yourself. Come down from the cross, if you really are the Son of God." The chief priests and the religious teachers and leaders of the nation insulted him as well. "He saved others, but he can't save himself," they mocked. "So he's the King of Israel? Let him come down from the cross and we'll believe him, and they quoted the Scripture: 'He trusted in God, now let him rescue him if he wishes,' for he said he was the Son of God." Even the rebels who were crucified with him added insults.

If this is not a direct quote it is a clear reference to Psalm 22:8. *"He trusts in the Lord,"* they say, *"let the Lord rescue him. Let him deliver him, since he delights in him."* In quoting Psalm 22, the priests were saying that Jesus is not the Son of God because in Psalm 22:24 God does deliver this suffering one (the Messiah) from his suffering. What they do not realize is that God will rescue him as he raises him from the dead.

45-56. As they waited, darkness came upon the land – from noon to three in the afternoon. About three in the afternoon Jesus cried loudly, "Eli, Eli, lema sabachthani?"[1] (Translated from Hebrew this means "My God, My God, why have you left me alone.")

This is the only verse from Psalm 22 quoted directly: "*My God, my God, why have you forsaken me? Why are you so far from saving me, so far from my cries of anguish?*" (verse 1) It settles the fact that the crucifixion is described in Psalm 22.

The connection of the crucifixion to Psalm 22 is so important that Jewish apologists (defenders of Judaism and the rejection of Jesus as Messiah) have gone to extensive lengths to argue that it does not connect. One good example is *Psalm 22 - "Nailing" An Alleged Crucifixion Scenario*. The argument is very involved and depends on differences between particular Hebrew words and the translations of them in the English Bible. But the argument is nit-picky and fails to convince that Psalm 22 is not connected to the crucifixion.

The author makes one good point, however, and that is that the psalm relates directly to King David and describes his experience. Christians would not disagree. We simply believe that the psalm has a prophetic meaning as well, and the many connections to Matthew twenty-seven confirm that.

Some who were there waiting for his death said, "He's calling for Elijah."

Then someone ran to get a sponge and filled it with sour wine vinegar. He put it on a staff and raised it up to Jesus that he could drink. The rest told him, "Leave him alone. Maybe Elijah will come to help him."

Jesus was thirsty. Psalm 22:15." *My mouth is dried up like a potsherd, and my tongue sticks to the roof of my mouth; you lay me in the dust of death.*"

But Jesus cried out again and gave up his spirit and died.

Execution by crucifixion usually took days. (It was supposed to.) It involved a severe beating that weakened the victim but was not intended to kill him. The purpose was to frighten anyone else who might be inclined to violate Roman law. That Jesus died so quickly was a surprise to the Roman soldiers who were in charge of the crucifixion.

The conclusion we come to is that Jesus was crucified but was not killed by the crucifixion. He literally gave up his life as Matthew said. His life was not taken from him; he gave it up as a sacrifice for us.

At that moment the curtain that divided the holy place from the most holy place in the Temple tore in two. There was a great earthquake that broke the rocks. (Many graves of holy people opened, and after the resurrection of Jesus they were raised to life and went into the holy city Jerusalem where many saw them.) When the Roman officer and the soldiers with him saw the earthquake and what was happening they were struck with fear. "He really was a son of God," they said.

Many of the women who had followed Jesus from Galilee and had cared for his needs were there and watching from

a distance. Among them were Mary from Magdala, Mary the mother of James and Joseph, and the mother of James and John, Zebedee's sons.

Some of the disciples were there as well. Certainly John was because he writes of Jesus telling him to take care of Mary.

57-61. When sundown drew near, Joseph came to the site of the crucifixion. He was a rich man from Arimathea, a man who had become a disciple of Jesus. Seeing Jesus dead he went to Pilate and asked for Jesus' body. Pilate gave the order that it be given to him, and Joseph took the body, wrapped it in a new linen cloth, and placed it in his own grave, which had newly been carved out of the rock. He then rolled the rock that sealed the grave in front of the entrance and went away. Mary from Magdala and the other Mary were there to watch the burial.

Burial was important for Jews, even if the man was a criminal. The body of an executed man was usually given to his relatives who would bury it that day - without ceremony. But instead, Jesus was buried in a rich man's grave. That must have seriously irritated the Jewish authorities, but it did more than that; it fulfilled Isaiah 53:9.

62-66. The next day, the day that followed the Day of Preparation, the leading priests and the Pharisees went to Pilate and asked, "Sir, we remember that this deceiver said while he was alive that after three days he would rise from the dead. So give an order that the grave be made secure with a guard until the third day. Otherwise his disciples may come and steal the body and say that he has been raised from the dead. That deception would be worse than the first."

The day after the Day of Preparation would have been a holy day, the first day of the Feast of Unleavened Bread. It would have been a Sabbath, though not necessarily the seventh day Sabbath. (By most reckonings it was also the seventh day Sabbath.) As on the seventh day Sabbath, no work was to be done. It speaks to how serious these priests saw the threat of the body being stolen and the claim that Jesus had risen from the dead. It was so serious that they would go to Pilate on such a holy day.

"I will give you a guard," Pilate said. "Go ahead and make it secure." So they put a seal on the tomb and posted the guard and made it as secure as they could.

Only Matthew, of the four Gospel writers, recorded the guards at the tomb. Some critics have suggested that Matthew created this story and that it did not happen and that it was not part of the oral history of Jesus and the crucifixion. But the particular audience to whom Matthew wrote suggests that the story is factual.

Matthew's directed his Gospel to Jewish readers in Syria and the Middle East. These people would have heard some of the oral stories. They would certainly have heard the Jewish version that the disciples stole the body of Jesus from the grave to make it look like he had risen from the dead. They would expect any story of the crucifixion to include this report. They also would not believe a report that did not fit with the oral stories. If it were not true, they of all people would know.

Matthew provided the background to the rumor that the disciples stole the body, and he provided detail that affirms the reports of the disciples and Apostles that had been circulating since the crucifixion.

FOOTNOTES

1. Both Matthew and Mark included these words of Jesus from the cross, and both translated them. That presents a puzzle. Why include the words in Hebrew/Aramaic (they are a combination of both) then translate rather than simply translate them as they did with all the rest of Jesus' words? It is probably because of the intensity of emotion captured in the Hebrew/Aramaic words and missing from the Greek translation. It is a common thing for speakers of several languages to use a phrase from one language, even if their hearers do not know it, because it expresses what they wish to say better than a translation. I may sometimes say *hasta la vista* (Spanish) when I want to express goodbye because it carries, in my mind, a slightly sarcastic tone compared to the English. These words of Jesus were remarkably laden with emotion both when spoken and as the disciples heard them. Including them in Aramaic conveys that emotion to the reader.

Chapter 28

The King Always

Christ's Appearance to Mary Magdalene after the Resurrection
by Alexander Ivanov (1806 - 1858), via Wikimedia Commons.

In his final word, Matthew recorded the mission the Messiah Jesus gives to all who are his disciples: As you go, make disciples. I am with you always.

This would have been especially significant to Matthew's readers. As Jewish Christians, they were already scattered. They were sojourners across the world. (That is how both Peter and James described them in 1 Peter and James.) And with the destruction of Jerusalem, they would have no homeland. But they had a commission. It was to make disciples of the Messiah. And that is what they did.

In time, the Jewish church was eclipsed by the many people from the nations who heard the message of the Messiah and believed on him. They, too, would take up the mission. And so it has been through the years since Jesus spoke those words. We who are followers of the Messiah Jesus, both Jews and people of the nations, have the job and the joy of being message-bearers.

1-10. After the Sabbath, early in the morning of the first day,[1] Mary from Magdala and the other Mary returned to the grave. As they were on their way, there was a violent earthquake, for an angel of the Lord came from heaven and rolled away the stone that was at the entrance of the tomb and sat on it. He looked like lightning; his clothes were as white as snow. The guards were terrified and shook with fear and became like dead men.

Why weren't the disciples all at the grave on this third day after Jesus' death? This would be the greatest day in history.

It is not that the disciples did not have plenty of notice. Jesus had spoken of his resurrection many times. It was that they didn't understand and couldn't believe that Jesus would die. They might have fought for him when he was alive, but when he died, that was the end for them. It was over. This crazy hope that Jesus would be the King of a new Kingdom was over. It was time to go home. Even the women were not there at his grave to be spectators of the resurrection. They were there to anoint a dead body. And then they would go home, back to life before Jesus. Except that it didn't happen that way.

But the angel said to the women, "Don't be afraid. I know you are looking for Jesus who was executed on the cross. He is not here, for he has risen as he said he would. Come see where the Lord lay. Then go quickly to tell his disciples that he is raised from the dead and that he is going ahead of you to Galilee. You will see him there. Now I have told you."

No one is much interested in a dead Messiah. If Jesus lies still in his tomb, the whole message of Matthew is meaningless. Jesus is not the King. He is not the Prophet. He is not the Priest. He is not the Savior. He is not the Messiah. He is history.

But if he is alive from the dead and lives now and forever, everything Matthew wrote of him and everything Jesus said of himself is true. For Matthew's Jewish readers the fact of the resurrection was like a tsunami. It changed the whole landscape of life.

When they heard this from the angel, they left quickly, both frightened and filled with great joy. But as they were on their way to tell the disciples, Jesus met them and said, "God's grace to you!" Recognizing his greeting, they fell down before him and took hold of his feet and worshiped him. Then Jesus said to them, "Don't be afraid. Go and give this message to my brothers: 'Go to Galilee. There you will see me.'"

"Seeing is believing." The disciples would surely have been justified in not believing that this miracle had happened if there had been no living Jesus as proof. But they saw him. All eleven of the disciples saw him. The women saw him. And the record of Paul in First Corinthians fifteen is that many, many others saw him.

And seeing him changed their lives. Before, they had been afraid and in hiding. Afterward, they were bold and fearless. Before, they had no message of the Kingdom of God; it had vanished with Jesus' death. Afterward, they had a message. Boy, did they have a message! They had a message of forgiveness, a message of God's love, a message of triumph over death, and a message of everlasting life for all who would follow the risen Messiah Savior King.

Every single one of these men and women went to their deaths convinced of this truth. After all, they had seen the living resurrected Jesus. Why wouldn't they believe it?

Of the eleven disciples, ten died because they believed and preached that Jesus was alive and was the living Savior Messiah. Why would anyone die for a lie that they knew to be a lie? No one would. No. They died for believing and preaching what they knew to be true and to be so important that living for it and dying for it was nothing in comparison.

But we have not seen the risen Jesus. How can we be sure?

We can be sure on the testimony of those who saw him and wrote about him. They are reliable witnesses; they had a reputation for honesty and reported only what they saw. As witnesses they all agreed; there are variations in their reports, but no disagreement to the fact of the resurrection. As witnesses they gained nothing by their testimony - except rejection by their own people, except suffering and death. In any court of law, they would be believed. We can be sure.

11-15. As the women continued on to the disciples with this message, some of the guards, who had gone into the city, went to the chief priests and told them all that had happened. The chief priests then met with the Jewish leaders and talked about what to do. Finally they gave the soldiers money and instructed them to tell people "His disciples came and stole the body while we were sleeping." Then they assured the soldiers, "If Pilate hears of this, we will keep you out of trouble."

This became the story that the priests told: The disciples stole the body. It was the story that was repeated over and over as the Jewish answer to the preaching that Jesus had risen from the dead. Matthew's Jewish readers must have heard it.

But it is the most improbable of stories. The disciples had no motive for stealing the body; they did not believe or anticipate Jesus' resurrection. They would have had no opportunity; the grave was well guarded. And they were afraid for their own lives; even had there been no guards at the tomb, they were afraid. That the women went to the tomb alone is evidence that the men were either too despondent or too afraid to go, even to pay their respects to Jesus' body, guards or no guards.

The only evidence the Jews provided for the stolen body was the testimony of the guards. But how could that have been believed? Were the guards actually asleep? Unlikely. Had they been sleeping on duty, that would have been a death sentence for them. Even if they were Jewish soldiers, they were under orders from Pilate. Were they over powered by the disciples? Unlikely. They did not return injured and beat up. And for guards to have not fought to the last man on the orders of their superiors was also a death sentence. And how could the disciples have stolen the body without waking the guards had they been asleep? Unlikely.

16-20. So the eleven disciples went to the mountain in Galilee where Jesus told them he would meet them. There

they saw him and bowed before him and worshiped him, though they still were troubled about what to think.

For the disciples this must have been a time of deep questioning. The conviction that Jesus was the Messiah King whom the Hebrew Scriptures had predicted was solid. But then their hopes in him and in the Kingdom were shattered by his death. And now he is alive again! But despite their joy in that, they had to have been troubled. Their worldview had been turned upside down so many times in the three years since Jesus had called them to follow him that they had not had time to catch up. What now? Where now? They did not know.

It is the same for everyone who comes to the realization that Jesus was and is the Messiah, that he is risen from the dead, that he lives as the King and the Lord of all. It turns their world upside down, and it takes time to reorient to a reality that is different, entirely different.

But Jesus spoke to encourage them. "All authority both in heaven and on earth has been given to me. As you go from this place,[2] make disciples of people from all nations. Baptize them in the Name – God the Father, God the Son, and God the Holy Spirit. Teach these new disciples to follow my instructions for living. And be confident of this, I will be with you always wherever you go, from now to the end of history."

These were marching orders for the disciples. And this is what they did. Peter went west to Rome. John went north to Syria and Turkey. James preached to the Jews in Jerusalem. Thomas went east to India. Matthew went first to Jews in Syria and then east to Jewish communities in Iraq, Iran and beyond. The destinations of the others are not as certain, but by 70 A.D. all those who were still living were scattered around the Roman Mediterranean world and beyond.

These are our marching orders as well: As you go, wherever you are and wherever God takes you, make disciples. Only this question remains. Will you?

FOOTNOTES

1. By Jewish reckoning the day begins at sundown, so this was actually half-way through the day.

2. Many translations make this a command. But it is really an assumption. It is assumed that these men would be going.

Postscript

Thus ends Matthew's story of the Messiah. This Gospel has been his argument, presented first to his Jewish readers and then passed on to us: JESUS IS MESSIAH AND SAVIOR. Matthew from beginning to end presented evidence and reason for believing that and for believing that Jesus lives today, still the Messiah and King and Savior and Lord.

The Gospel has been a call, using Jesus' own words: "Follow me." And it has been an explanation of what that means. It means following Jesus in his manner of life, and it means trust in him as Messiah and Savior. Those two cannot be separated. There is no true faith without following, and there is no true following without faith.

The act of faith and following is not described as a decision of a moment or a decision to be made without thinking through the implications. Following Jesus will bring hardship and will attract opposition. Following Jesus will mean giving up claim to personal wealth and an easy life; from the moment we begin to follow Jesus, we turn over to him ownership of those things. Following Jesus will mean obedience to him and to a life dedicated to right living.

But following Jesus has huge eternal rewards. It leads to LIFE, and it will take you on the adventure of a lifetime.

If you have read this handbook to the end, you are likely already a follower of Jesus. But if you are not, would you consider carefully becoming his follower? Once you have made that decision, you may just say YES to him; he hears you. Then follow.

Profile of Matthew

Knowing the author and his purpose in writing is important to the understanding of any piece of writing and certainly to our understanding of this Gospel. In fact, as we better understand the man called Matthew and his passion both for the Messiah and for his own Jewish people, what he wrote about Jesus takes on greater meaning.

Who was this Matthew? The traditional answer is that he was one of the disciples, the man called by Jesus to be one of the inner group of twelve disciples and the one whose calling is recorded in all three of the synoptic gospels (Matthew, Mark, and Luke). But in recent years that assumption has been challenged by some scholars. They point to the fact that the author, whoever he was, did not sign his name to the manuscript. If it had been Matthew the disciple and Apostle, attaching his name to the Gospel would have given it greater credibility. Wouldn't he have done that?

Secondly, the author includes no first person "we" memories of Jesus or any personal recollections that today we would expect of an author who shared three years with Jesus and the other disciples. Why are there no passages like this one from the book of Acts where Luke describes his sea journey with Paul: "After three months *we* put out to sea in a ship that had wintered in the island"?

Finally, the author seems to use long passages from a previously existing source rather than personal eyewitness testimony – which the author must have had if he were the disciple Matthew. So, were we mistaken? I do not think so.

Consider who Matthew was. He was a sinner, a tax collector, a nobody. If we were to ask him about himself, that is what he would have said, and that is what he did say. It was enough. The Gospel was not about him. It was about Jesus.

However, if we look more deeply into the Gospel and at the evidence from the early church fathers, there is more than this brief portrait.

The first piece of evidence is the words of the early church father Papias. Writing in the early part of the second century, Papias identifies the author of the book as the Apostle Matthew. Papias also tells us that Matthew was the first to write the sayings (*logia*) of Jesus and that he wrote for Jewish Christians and wrote originally in the Hebrew or Aramaic language.[1] That agrees with others who wrote about the Gospel and about Matthew a little later. And it agrees with the evidence in the book itself. Though the text we have is in Greek, there are remnants of a Hebrew original in the Greek text. One easily seen example is the way the author wrote the history of Jesus' family in chapter one. Compared to Luke's history, Matthew's is very much like the genealogies of the Old Testament. In other words, it sounds Hebrew, even though written in Greek.[2]

Many modern scholars dismiss Papias as unreliable. But Papias lived only a generation after the Apostles. He spoke with men who had personally known some of the Apostles. To Papias, Matthew was more than a name from history. He was a real person and a respected Apostle. To take the word of someone who lived so close to the life of the author seems reasonable. He certainly knew the events surrounding the beginning of the church far better than we can know them from a distance of almost two thousand years.

The second line of evidence is the manual for conduct and practice in the early church called *The Didache*. It is dated to the early second century (100-130 A.D.) and was considered by the early church to be the teachings of the Apostles. The *Didache* contains the Lord's Prayer just as it appears in Matthew's Gospel and the formula used for baptizing – "in the name of the Father, Son, and Holy Spirit" – found in chapter twenty-eight of the Gospel. Along with these quotes, *The Didache* also uses many briefer phrases and words of Jesus from the Sermon on the Mount not found in any other Gospel. The heavy dependence of *The Didache* on Matthew would indicate both the early and apostolic origin of Matthew's Gospel. It also testifies to the importance of the Gospel to the early church. There is really no reason to look further than the Apostle Matthew for the author. In fact, no one up to the last century did. There was simply no other author suggested in any of the sources in the early centuries.

However, it is not the testimony of history that is most important. It is the portrait of Matthew that emerges from the book itself that recommends the authorship of Matthew most strongly.

The author was clearly a literate and knowledgeable reader of the Hebrew Scriptures. He quoted extensively from those Scriptures, more than any of the other three gospel writers. And his knowledge is understandable when we see in the Gospels of Mark and Luke that Matthew was also known as Levi. That name identifies Matthew as a man belonging to the family clan assigned to serve in temple ministry, and that implies that Matthew would have been a man well schooled in the Scriptures of Israel.

Yet when we are introduced to him in the Gospels he was not in the temple. He was working at the most despised of professions, a tax collector for Herod and the Romans, and consorting with sinners. How had he fallen?

Perhaps Matthew's personal experience of the "religion" of Israel is the answer.

Matthew would have grown up in a family intimately associated with religion. He would have personally seen the corruption and political compromise and deadness that Jesus confronted and Matthew reported at length in the Gospel. If he had been a young man serious about God, dead religion close up and personal must have been a terrible, disturbing disappointment. Like many young people today who have become disillusioned by the emptiness of the religion they see in churches, the only option seemed to be to walk away from it all. He didn't end up pouring drinks in a sleazy back street bar, but his job as tax collector and partier with sinners was not much different. It was as far away from the religion of his youth as he could get. Yet there smoldered in Matthew a hope. It was a passion that is evident in his frequent references to the prophet Isaiah.

Isaiah, more than any other prophet, weeps in pain at the moral and spiritual decline of Israel. Yet this same Isaiah deeply hopes in the promised Messiah – whose portrait he so wonderfully draws in the fifty-third chapter of his message. For Isaiah, Messiah is the Servant of God who would take away the sin of his people whom he pictured as an "afflicted city" (Isaiah 54:11) and a people who were waiting in "darkness" (Isaiah 61:1). And that was Matthew. He was a pile of dry kindling waiting for a flame. Jesus was that flame.

Jesus came preaching that the Kingdom of God was here. It was now. And Jesus demonstrated it with the power of his words and his acts. The Messiah Isaiah had spoken of had come, and Matthew was convinced deep down and without question that Jesus was the hope of Israel. Jesus was the Messiah! It must have sent a chill down his back when Matthew first came to that realization.

Matthew's passionate surrender to the one he knew to be Messiah left him forever humbled. It is telling that Matthew alone used the name *Matthew* and not Levi when he tells of his own calling to follow Jesus. The other two gospel writers called him Levi. But the name Levi carried far more status than Matthew wished to bear. Forever after he would call himself simply "a man named Matthew" (Matthew 9:9).

It is also telling that in the list of the twelve disciples included in all three of the synoptic Gospels, Matthew alone would add to his name "the tax collector." He might as well have written Matthew the sinner, for that was what he meant. Yes, Matthew's encounter with Messiah left him deeply and profoundly humbled, but it also left him with a burden.

Matthew's passionate surrender to Messiah would turn him to his people with the message that had so changed his life, the message of a Servant Savior. He saw his people as the people described by Isaiah:

Like the blind we grope along the wall, feeling our way like people without eyes. At Midday we stumble as if it were twilight; among the strong, we are like the dead. (Isaiah 59:10)

Upon them the light had now dawned. And with the burden of a prophet, Matthew would spend the rest of his life speaking the message of Messiah Jesus, the Light. He would bear that burden to his people in Judea and then across western Asia. Out of that passion flow the words of the book we know as the Gospel of Matthew.

1. *Fragments of Papias, VI.* New Advent. Newadvent.org.

2. Matthew uses the word *egennesen* to express the idea of *gave birth to*. Some English translations translate that as *begat* as in "Abraham begat Isaac." (See Genesis 5:4 for the use of *egennesen* in the Greek Septuagint version of the Old Testament.) That is the usual way this relationship is expressed in the Hebrew idiom. Luke on the other hand describes the relationship of son to father in the usual Greek idiom using the genitive *tou* as in "Isaac the one of Abraham."

History of the Gospel of Matthew

Date of writing. Various dates have been proposed for the writing of Matthew's Gospel. Liberal scholars often propose a late first century date, sometime after the destruction of Jerusalem in 70 A.D. The thinking seems to be that the author was not personally acquainted with Jesus' life and therefore must have written later rather than earlier.

But a late dating of Matthew's Gospel is based on the assumption that Matthew used Mark's Gospel as a source and, therefore, it had to have been written some time after Mark. I will consider whether Mark was a source for Matthew in the next section. For the moment, I question that assumption.

The evidence, however, from the church fathers writing in second century, particularly Papias and Origen, is that the Gospel of Matthew was written during the time when Peter and Paul were in Rome. That would point to a date of A.D. 50 to 64.

From the evidence in the book itself a date prior to the Jewish Roman war and the destruction of Jerusalem and of the temple in 70 A.D. seems probable. The best evidence for a pre-70 date is the passage in chapter twenty-three in which Jesus condemns the Pharisees for their hypocrisy.

The church had been struggling with the legalism of the Pharisees during the time of Paul's ministry in the 50s. Paul wrote several of his letters, Romans and Galatians, to argue against the Jewish rules these Pharisees were trying to impose on non-Jewish believers. He made a special trip to Jerusalem to confer with the leaders of the church there regarding the problems the Pharisees were creating for believers. And he went away from that first church council with the agreement that the legalism of these Pharisees was not to be imposed on non-Jewish believers. It was a serious issue.

Matthew, writing to Jewish believers, would have had similar concerns. The many encounters of Jesus with the Pharisees, especially in the twenty-third chapter, fit the historical context of a mid-50s date better than they do a later date when the influence of the Pharisees was almost non-existent and the separation between Judaism and the followers of Jesus was nearly complete.

Additionally, the prophecy in chapter twenty-four regarding the destruction of the temple would seem to have been unnecessary. The temple would already have been destroyed. The prophecy would not then have been a prophecy with any importance to the readers. It would have simply been a reminder that Jesus had foretold the temple's destruction. But if that were the case, we might expect Matthew to make that point as he did with other fulfilled prophecies. As a fulfilled prophecy, it would have provided greater credibility for the part of the prophecy yet unfulfilled. But he does not.

When all the evidence is considered, a date earlier than 70 A.D. and perhaps between 50 and 65 A.D. is likely.

Sources. Everyone who reads the Gospels notices the similarity among the first three: Matthew, Mark and Luke. Scholars use the term *synoptic* to describe that similarity. The term means that they share a similar point of view and pattern of organization, or plot. [1]

What scholars mean by "point of view" is that Jesus is portrayed as the Messiah anticipated in the Old Testament: as a king, as a preacher, and as a worker of miracles. His portrayal also as the Son of God is of secondary emphasis. In contrast, the Gospel of John first and foremost portrays Jesus as the eternal Word and the Son of God.

I should note that John, writing in the last decade of the first century, wrote to refute the growing controversy about the nature of Christ. The issue was not whether Jesus was the Messiah. That would have been of secondary concern to the largely non-Jewish churches to whom John wrote. The issue was whether Jesus was God the Son. For Matthew, on the other hand, writing before the destruction of Jerusalem to a largely Jewish church, the issue was whether Jesus was the Messiah.

By organization scholars mean that the synoptic Gospels follow the story of Jesus' life beginning in Galilee and ending in Jerusalem with many events taking place in the same locations and contexts in all three. John, on the other hand, focuses on Jesus in Jerusalem and does not include many of the events or teaching of Jesus included in the other Gospels.

But there is far more shared by these three Gospels than viewpoint and plot. When we read carefully, there is a lot of similarity in the little stories (called pericopae) that are included in the larger narrative of the gospels.

Look at the story of the calling of Matthew in Matthew 9:9-13; Mark 2:13-17; and Luke 5:27-32. Except for minor differences, they look very much alike. In other passages the shared stories are even more similar, being word for word the same, even in the Greek text. How did that happen?

There are three possibilities suggested today. One possibility is that one of the gospels was used by the other two writers as a source for the stories, for the words of Jesus, and for the basic organization of the life of Jesus. In other words, the writers of two of the gospels copied from the source Gospel. That Gospel is often considered today to have been Mark, and the hypothesis is called the

Markan priority. This proposal is based on two facts. First, almost all of Mark is used in Matthew or Luke and the organizational patterns of Matthew and Luke follow Mark's pattern. Second, Mark is the shortest and has the least amount of narrative supplied by the author. It is argued that an author would not reduce the information in the source but increase it by the addition of more narrative or commentary. Hence, Mark did not copy from Matthew or Luke, but because Matthew and Luke enlarge upon the story in Mark, they must have used Mark as a source.

The problem is that both Matthew and Luke share pericopae that are not in Mark. That observation has led some scholars to suggest a second source which Matthew and Luke used but Mark did not. This is called the two-source hypothesis and is the second possibility. There is even the idea that there were three sources, and that brings us to the third possibility.

It is possible that there was a source that included the sayings of Jesus and was written prior to the writing of any of the Gospels. Matthew, Mark, and Luke then each drew from that source using the stories that fit their rhetorical purpose to compose their Gospels. Sometimes that source is called Q, which stands for *Quelle* meaning source in German.

The idea of an earlier source does make sense. Luke, at the beginning of his Gospel makes reference to the sources he used (1:1-4). He says that his sources were "those who from the first were eyewitnesses and servants of the word." That would sound like Luke was relying on the accounts, either oral or written, of the Apostles and perhaps others. That is an intriguing idea, and I'll come back to that later. But we can imagine there were many remembered stories of Jesus. Many people heard him and saw his miracles and later became followers. These stories certainly were passed on orally if not in written form.

A second reason for concluding there was an original source for the Gospels is that the words of Jesus are not at all like the narrative framework provided by the Gospel writers. Jesus' words bear strong indicators in all of the Gospels of distinctly Hebrew idioms, called Hebraisms. These have not been reworked into the Greek idiom as a modern translator might but are literal translations from a Hebrew original source. In contrast the narrative framework supplied by the gospel writers, such as the birth narratives in Matthew and Luke and the narrative of the baptism in Mark and the narrative matrix that fills out the stories appear to have been written originally in Greek by fluent Greek speaking writers. (Both Matthew and Luke are written in very good Greek. Mark less so.) That suggests there was a source for these sayings of Jesus outside the Gospels.

What are the clues that point us to the source?

We read in Acts 2:42 that from the earliest days of the church the new disciples gathered to hear the "apostles' teaching." That phrase in Greek is *te didache* and means the body of truth taught by the Apostles. Though we are not told specifically in Acts what those truths were, it is expected that they were the stories about Jesus and his teachings. Those stories might have been quickly arranged as easily remembered pieces so that they could be repeated. These became, along with the Hebrew Scriptures, the "Bible" for the early church. They were probably orally transmitted and were repeated often at first, which was common in a culture where only a few could read. But they may have been written down as well. Certainly they were finally written down by the Gospel writers. If they were transcribed by different scribes at different times and places, it is certainly possible that slight variations of wording would have become a part of the written stories. That may well be why the synoptic Gospels have so many stories in common, yet not always word for word the same. The Olivet Discourse in Matthew 24, Mark 13, and Luke 21 is one example of the same story told differently.

That body of oral and written material served the church for several decades before the Gospel writers used them in their Gospels, and that is what Luke referred to in the early verses of his Gospel as the accounts of "those who were eyewitness and servants of the word." They were the teaching of the apostles'. If so and if Matthew was one of the apostles, these stories would essentially be his eyewitness accounts.

Each of the Gospel writers also customized their narrative to fit his target audience. Mark adds explanations of Jewish customs and translations of some Hebrew terms which his Roman readers would not understand. Matthew added many quotes from the Hebrew Scriptures that would be of significance for his Jewish audience.

Matthew also, alone of the three, personalized some of what he wrote. For instance, whereas all three synoptic gospel writers included the story of the calling of Levi (Matthew) the tax collector, only the writer Matthew used "Matthew" as the name. And only Matthew added in the list of the twelve disciples that Matthew was the tax collector and the one who gave the feast for his tax collector friends· after his calling. That personalization is the best clue to the Gospel's author, Matthew.

However, the core of the story of Matthew's (Levi's) calling and the list of the twelve disciples is the same in all three gospels. And that holds true for all the shared stories. The only possible conclusion is that they shared a common source and that source was not one of the Gospels. That shared source is best identified as the teaching of the apostles.

It seems that Q, for which many have been looking, has been hiding in plain sight in the Gospels of Matthew, Mark, and Luke. Q is the teaching of the apostles collected and taught in the early church.

1. White, L. Michael. "From Jesus to Christ." Frontline. PBS, April 1998. Web 13 Feb. 2016.

Recipients. There is no question among Bible scholars that the Gospel of Matthew was directed toward Jewish Christians and toward others of the Jewish people. His regular use of the Hebrew Scriptures and the lack of explanation of Jewish traditions, explanations that would be expected if non-Jews were to be his readers and which we do find in the Gospel of Mark, direct us to that conclusion. But among these, to whom specifically did he write?

The answer comes from the church fathers. According to these men and their memories of the early church, Matthew worked first among his own people. His audience would have included believers in Jerusalem, but his audience extended to congregations of primarily Jewish Christians beyond, in Judea and as far as Antioch in Syria.

Then during the time when Paul and Peter were in Rome (50 to 65 A.D.) Matthew was moved to extend his ministry east into Asia. (Tradition tells us that Christians in northern India had copies of Matthew's Gospel. That would suggest that he did indeed travel east and that he took his Gospel with him.) The early church fathers tell us that for the sake of those well-beloved Jewish believers in Jesus he was leaving behind, and that they might have a written testimony to the Lord Jesus, Matthew composed his Gospel, and perhaps as Papias indicates, he composed it first in the Hebrew language. I can easily imagine that to be so and that these groups of Jewish Christians in Jerusalem and Syria and Antioch were the first to benefit from his work.

Purpose. Matthew's purpose in writing was to tell his people the story of Jesus the Messiah. Those readers included, first of all, the Jewish church in Jerusalem and Judea and then those scattered throughout the world. They would need a record of the Messiah's life and message as the years went forward. The Apostles who had been the teachers in Jerusalem, including James the brother of Jesus and Peter, were already scattered – or dead, as was James the brother of John. Matthew himself was moving on to tell the story in new regions. A written record of Jesus would be essential for the church he was leaving behind. But the messages in chapter twenty-four and twenty-eight suggest that it was also Matthew's purpose to encourage these believers. According to Jesus, Jerusalem and their homeland would be destroyed. They would be scattered throughout the world. But Jesus promised to be with them wherever they traveled. It was a promise that they would need to hold on to in hard times.

Significance

Matthew's Gospel is the completion of the Old Testament Hebrew Scriptures. It completes the picture of the Messiah, whose revealing had been the whole aim of the Old Testament. In the Gospel of Matthew, Jesus is the seed of the woman who would crush the head of the serpent, promised in Genesis 3:15, He is the one who would bless all the nations of the earth, promised to Abraham in Genesis 12:2,3.. He is Shiloh who will be King forever, predicted in Genesis 49:10. He is the prophet who will speak unto us the words of God, promised by Moses in Deuteronomy 18:18. He is the Servant and sacrifice who was wounded for our transgressions in Isaiah 53:5. He is the "Wonderful Counselor, the Mighty God, the Everlasting Father, the Prince of Peace" in Isaiah 9:6.

It is wholly right that Matthew's Gospel should come first in the New Testament. It is the bridge to all that follows. It connects the first part of God's story to the last. Without The Gospel of Matthew the New Testament would seem like a new and different story. With Matthew, it is the completion of the story begun long ago and only now coming to its completion.

For those who want to use this book in a group study, there are free study guides available on the author's website:

http://drcpublishing.net

96413177R00133

Made in the USA
Columbia, SC
26 May 2018